Cambridge Elements ≡

Elements in Public and Nonprofit Administration
edited by
Andrew Whitford
University of Georgia
Robert Christensen
Brigham Young University

CALIBRATING PUBLIC ACCOUNTABILITY

The Fragile Relationship between Police Departments and Civilians in an Age of Video Surveillance

Daniel E. Bromberg
University of New Hampshire

Étienne Charbonneau
École nationale d'administration publique

CAMBRIDGE
UNIVERSITY PRESS

University Printing House, Cambridge CB2 8BS, United Kingdom

One Liberty Plaza, 20th Floor, New York, NY 10006, USA

477 Williamstown Road, Port Melbourne, VIC 3207, Australia

314–321, 3rd Floor, Plot 3, Splendor Forum, Jasola District Centre, New Delhi – 110025, India

79 Anson Road, #06–04/06, Singapore 079906

Cambridge University Press is part of the University of Cambridge.

It furthers the University's mission by disseminating knowledge in the pursuit of education, learning, and research at the highest international levels of excellence.

www.cambridge.org
Information on this title: www.cambridge.org/9781108963992
DOI: 10.1017/9781108966658

First published 2021

A catalogue record for this publication is available from the British Library.

ISBN 978-1-108-96399-2 Paperback
ISSN 2515-4303 (online)
ISSN 2515-429X (print)

Additional resources for this publication at www.cambridge.org/bromberg

Calibrating Public Accountability

The Fragile Relationship between Police Departments and Civilians in an Age of Video Surveillance

Elements in Public and Nonprofit Administration

DOI: 10.1017/9781108966658
First published online: March 2021

Daniel E. Bromberg
University of New Hampshire

Étienne Charbonneau
École nationale d'administration publique

Author for correspondence: Daniel E. Bromberg, daniel.bromberg@unh.edu

Abstract: Accountability is a staple of Public Administration scholarship, but scholars have been unsuccessful in developing a predictive model of accountable behavior. Large swaths of research about accountability still focus on scarcely read annual reports as video footage of police encounters are watched and discussed by citizens regularly. In this Element, we seek to further a predictive model of accountability by understanding the norms and expectations associated with the implementation of body-worn cameras. Specifically, this research examines when police departments release, or do not release, footage to the public and the expectations civilians have about the release of that footage. Indirectly, the norms and expectations associated with this technology have broad implications for societal values and the relationship between civilians and law enforcement. Our findings suggest the relationship between law enforcement and civilians is central to the implementation of this policy and, more broadly, accountability.

Keywords: accountability, body-worn cameras, experimental video vignette, law enforcement, surveillance, transparency, trust

ISBNs: 9781108963992 (PB), 9781108966658 (OC)
ISSNs: 2515-4303 (online), 2515-429X (print)

Contents

1 Introduction: The Tales of Body-Worn Cameras' Accountability and Trust

Conventional wisdom about police culture has long been shaped by what people consume on their televisions. From *Cops* to *NYPD Blue* to *Law & Order* to *The Wire*, people have come to understand police culture as filtered through the lens of a camera. Yet, while we still have police dramas on television, we no longer need Hollywood to provide us with this fictional lens.

Today, we have thousands of cameras worn on the bodies of police officers showing real footage of police actions. Added to that mix is the onslaught of individuals armed with their cell phones, who capture police behavior as officers go about their daily routines. Police culture is no longer understood through the eyes of Andy Sipowicz or Jimmy McNulty. For better or worse, Michael Slager and Daniel Pantaleo define it. Eric Garner and Sandra Bland define it. George Floyd defines it.

Since the shooting of Michael Brown in 2016, police departments across the United States have outfitted their officers with body-worn cameras (BWCs). While the use of BWC technology in the United States precedes this watershed moment (White and Malm 2020, p. 4), Brown's shooting caused an acceleration effect that drove its rapid expansion. Law enforcement agencies in the United States soon caught up to police departments in the United Kingdom, which first tested BWCs in 2005 (Bowling and Iyer 2019, p. 144). This technology provides a rare example of widespread acceptance, as citizen groups, legal defense organizations like the America Civil Liberties Union (ACLU), and law enforcement have all called for its implementation (Fan 2018, p. 1654). The common goal of BWC programs is to enhance transparency, which it is assumed will lead to greater accountability – itself seen as naturally enhancing legitimacy (Chavis 2019, p. 453). Similar forces were at play in the late 1980s and 1990s after the 1991 beating of Rodney King in Los Angeles, which was followed by the acceleration of patrol cruisers being equipped with dashcams (Pagliarella 2016, pp. 534–535).

The assumption that BWCs or greater transparency will lead to accountability is "confusing the normative (that which our democratic values lead us to believe in) with the analytical (that which the social sciences allow us to claim)" (Fox 2007, p. 665). Police chiefs and politicians touting the benefits of BWC readily share this unproven assumption. Take, for example, recent comments by US Congressman Greg Stanton – former mayor of Phoenix and sponsor of the COPS Accountability Act of 2020. In reference to the nationwide implementation of BWC, Stanton said: "As we rethink 21st century policing, we have to make changes that can increase transparency and accountability to make everyone safer" (Office of Congressman Stanton, Media Office, July 2020). Large and small departments alike across the country are making similar comments. The finance director of Fort Smith, Arkansas, a police department historically reticent to use BWC, said, "Our department must be in line with the ideals of 21st-century policing, including the tenants of transparency and accountability of actions" (Watson 2018). These comments fail to address the many challenges associated with an accountability initiative such as BWCs. First, at the most basic level, as the Reporters Committee for Freedom of the Press's executive director recently commented, "Bodycams and dashcams cannot be effective tools for accountability if the public can never see the images they capture" (Lannan 2019). An official of the civil rights and technology nonprofit Upturn articulated a similar sentiment, suggesting that BWCs failed to deliver on accountability because the release of footage is often denied or delayed (Schlinkmann 2020). This concern relates to the second challenge, and the primary focus of this Element.

To whom is one accountable and for what must they account? These are two of the most fundamental questions in Public Administration literature, but they continue to challenge the discipline. Simplistic renderings of this complex landscape will provide false hope for authentic accountability. The challenge is not to articulate the many "for whoms" and "for whats" to which law enforcement is accountable. Rather, as BWCs are touted to the public as a tool for accountability, we aim to explain this accountable relationship. Public Administration has conveniently classified these criteria into a simple typology that encompasses both the "to whom" and "for what" one should be accountable. Bovens (2007) notes five forums that students of Public Administration will find very familiar: organizational accountability, political accountability, legal accountability, administrative accountability, and professional accountability. Furthermore, police departments are held accountable for output measures like crimes, arrests, and clearance rates, rather than measures of outcomes: "Even in an era that stresses managerial accountability, the procedural justice with which officers act is typically not measured in police agencies, nor is it an outcome for which police managers are held accountable" (Worden and McLean 2017, p. 9). The over-reliance on structured forums with hard output measures does little to achieve authentic accountability. Rather, as Dubnick (2005) has pointed out, "Our misguided preoccupation with management as the heart and soul of modern governance is not only blinding us to such basic questions, but is also binding us to theories and models that continue to send us down the wrong path" (p. 402).

We need to place greater emphasis on the social relationships that form the foundation of accountability. Most empirical research on accountability focuses on lengthy administrative reports that citizens and politicians rarely read. In an age of unlimited information and constant technological advances, accountability takes on new characteristics. The rules of accountability that once existed primarily within the walls of a courthouse or were bound by a bureaucracy now exist on the streets of New York City, Chicago, Los Angeles, Minneapolis, and Ferguson. The emergence of BWCs, and other video technology, shapes newly imagined accountability standards. If our interpretation of accountability is valid, then it is necessary to understand expectations from both parties in the relationship to achieve accountability. In this effort, we collect data from both residents and police chiefs regarding perceptions that surround the release of BWC footage. This Element uses a combination of population-based survey experiments and qualitative inquiry to deepen our understanding of what police chiefs and US residents perceive to be a transparent and trustworthy sharing of BWC footage.

Outside of criminology, most emerging surveillance literature is found in the private sector, leaving a limited number of studies focused on the public sector (Kayas et al. 2019, p. 1171). While we borrow heavily from criminology literature, we focus on the implementation of a specific aspect of BWC policies: police BWC footage being released to the public. Therefore, we heed the caution of criminologists Michael White and Aili Malm (2020, p. 13), which will not surprise those in Public Administration: implementation is critically important.

One of the twelve grand challenges identified by the National Academy of Public Administration (2019) for the next decade is to "Ensure Data Security and Individual Privacy." One of the ways in which public agencies and public administrators can reach that goal is "ensuring that the regulatory framework is informed by the careful consideration of the ethical aspects of data collection and dissemination" (National Academy of Public Administration 2019). The data collection part of BWC has been documented copiously in law reviews and criminology journals. Public Administration, with its storied legacy of studying accountability, is well positioned to address the dissemination part of that great challenge for the 2020s.

Objectives: This Element focuses on the relationship between the public and their government. More specifically, it addresses a new tool of accountability and the expectations associated with its use: "If body-worn cameras are as valuable as some claim, it is important that the process of adoption within police departments be as effective and efficient as possible" (Jennings, Fridell, and Lynch 2014, p. 549). Research on BWCs has primarily been accomplished in the domain of criminology. While understandable, this has created a limited scope of questions that especially focus on the incidence of crimes and citizen complaints. Lum and Gest (2018) note that "although some research on body-worn cameras has emerged, most criminal justice technologies have not been evaluated enough for us to know whether they work to control crime or improve legitimacy, as well as what their unintended consequences are" (p. 267). In fact, "actual measurable improvement of accountability due to BWCs has been scarce" (White and Malm 2020, p. 22).

Thompson's (2019) ongoing project regarding elected police commissioners finds that broad, local left-right preferences are reflected with some styles of policing. However, the same might not be true for public support of specific policy decisions, spanning from a failure of elected officials and the courts to rein in police departments – Friedman's thesis in *Unwarranted: Policing without Permission* – to perceived societal pressure to express support for police forces (Bromberg, Charbonneau, and Smith 2018). This project will advance knowledge on public support and police chiefs' support for specific policy and management elements related to police accountability via the release of BWC video footage, rather than solely examining their support for the general idea of having police officers equipped with BWCs.

Context: Police departments do far more than keep the peace. They are one of the few public services open twenty-four hours a day. With time, their role has expanded and, in many cases, transformed officers into social workers, teachers, community organizers, and dogcatchers (Vitale 2018). This is not strictly an American phenomenon. In October 2019, two *Sûreté du Québec* police officers went to a Drummondville hospital employee's home after being called by a hospital manager to escort back an employee who had skipped his night shift (Bilodeau 2019). The phenomenon is analogous to what Brooks (2016) describes in her book, *How Everything Became War and the Military Became Everything: Tales from the Pentagon*, regarding how uniformed men and women with guns are asked to deal with missions that used to be the dominion of the civilian US State Department. The fact that police officers, trained as crime fighters, are called to be everything from social workers to warriors speaks to the myriad tasks they are expected to accomplish. This has not only increased the number of interactions police have with the public but also muddied the expectations of appropriate behavior. Since 2016, many of these interactions have been recorded with BWCs, allowing the public to view and evaluate said expectations.

As of 2018, about 50 percent of law enforcement agencies in the United States had adopted BWCs. There is a good deal of variation across the country with southern and western states having greater rates of adoption compared with northeastern states (Nix, Todak, and Tregle 2020). Nevertheless, this translates into millions of hours of footage (Kofman 2017). In the United States, police departments are among the public institutions with the highest levels of trust (Pew 2018); the same is true in Canada (Cotter 2015). Laws, policies, statutes, and directives about the use and release of video footage show a high level of heterogeneity in the United States (Urban Institute 2018). That could be due to the absence of strong and unifying video guidelines. One explanation is that there is significant discretion in the current environment, where many police departments must manage flows of video footage captured by BWCs and their policies reflect personal preferences. Some agencies decide to release footage; others decide to keep this data private, but what influences police chiefs' decisions to release footage to the public? What do US residents expect in terms of accessing the footage of police-citizen interactions filmed by BWCs? Police BWCs have gained popularity in recent years. However, many advocates minimize the complexity of this transparency initiative and elevate potential benefits. While BWCs can promote police accountability, they may also reduce citizen trust in police organizations. The way a law enforcement agency manages its video data plays a role in the relationship between citizens and police officers.

In the next section, we will discuss several accountability typologies, frameworks, and models. Shortcomings and limits will be pointed out. We will offer propositions stemming from a synthesis of the Social Psychology literature by Thomas Schillemans, which culminated with the development of the Calibrated Public Accountability Model. In Section 3, the first empirical section, we discuss our submission of an experimental video vignette about a fatal police shooting, having sent it to hundreds of US police chiefs. We examine whether the anticipated timing of accountability and trust plays a role in preferences for how to share BWC footage with the public. Section 4 examines the results of 4,000 Americans – 3,000 of them from three cities – answering a similar survey with the video vignette. We compare their preferences and perceptions of transparency among cities with those of police chiefs. In the last empirical section, Section 5, we discuss the results of having asked hundreds more police chiefs to offer a narrative about the effects of BWCs on their relationship with their stakeholders. We conclude the Element by looking at how BWCs and other surveillance technologies have changed the way accountability is lived in the public sector (Section 6).

BWC programs and policy options are often seen as technical, the antitheses of big questions (Ariel 2019, p. 502). And while this may be the case from a theoretical standpoint, technical decisions are often the most impactful. Just as Lipsky (1980) reminded us more than forty years ago, street-level decisions "mediate aspects of the constitutional relationship of the citizens to the state" (p. 4). Our aim, with this research, is to contribute to and advance the multitude of existing frameworks toward a middle-range public accountability theory, stemming from the use of technology in one public service: policing.

2 Accountability: Frameworks, Frameworks Everywhere

Introduction

Accountability presents a puzzling conceptual challenge. As concepts mature, the clarity of their meaning crystalizes. Researchers tend to coalesce around a concept before scholarly communities establish a working definition, a framework, and ultimately a theory by which to test propositions and hypotheses. In the Public Administration literature, accountability does not fit this mold. Rather, one might argue, just the opposite has happened. The concept has matured, but the path to developing theoretical models has become more convoluted. Empirically, examination of accountability has dramatically lagged in comparison to its conceptual manifestations. If this were simply an academic exercise, then one might let it linger in perpetuity as academics postulate and pontificate about conceptual bounds of this oft-used word. Accountability, however, lives outside the world of academics. It is part of everyday nomenclature and used by advocates, attorneys, legislators, police chiefs, school superintendents, and social workers along with countless other business executives and public servants. Following the death of George Floyd in Minneapolis, on June 8, 2020, the House of Representatives introduced a bill titled the George Floyd Justice in Policing Act of 2020. The summary text reads as follows:

> This bill addresses a wide range of policies and issues regarding policing practices and law enforcement accountability. It includes measures to increase accountability for law enforcement misconduct, to enhance transparency and data collection, and to eliminate discriminatory policing practices.

While the language of this summary text reads as if it were taken straight out of a Public Administration textbook, the reality is that our discipline can offer limited predictive empirical insights. For decades, Public Administration scholars have taken a Derridian approach – deconstructing every code and building conceptual frameworks but failing to capture the complex interrelated human processes required to understand and predict human behavior. As Schillemans and Busuioc (2015) note,

> These prevalent typologies of public accountability in the public administration literature are all *descriptive*. They are of great help in identifying different forms of accountability and also help in retrospect to make sense of – tragic or exemplary – decision-making or policy outcomes. However, these typologies are less suitable for *predictive* usage in terms of the design of accountability

mechanisms or the formulation of hypotheses for the study of the behavior of persons and organizations in accountability processes. (p. 194)

Hence, while Public Administration scholars might be able to diagnose the failures of the accountability systems in the murder of George Floyd, they can offer scant evidence from empirical studies within the field that would have saved his life.

Accountability Frameworks

Public accountability may be the most central concept in all of Public Administration, but the field has failed to develop a clear predictive theory. One may make many arguments as to why this has not happened; however, two dominant reasons are evident. First, many scholars have been satisfied with conceptual frameworks. Conceptual frameworks or typologies have an enduring place in the Public Adminstration canon. The frameworks of both Romzek and Dubnick (1987) and Bovens (2007) have more than 1,000 citations, with the latter having more than 2,000. Both of these frameworks have led to a proliferation of articles that examine the concept of accountability; while they have provided a foundation upon which a theory might be developed, that has never happened. Second, Public Administration scholars have been over-reliant on the principal-agent (P-A) theory as a predictive basis for accountable behavior. P-A theory has its supporters and offers some flexibility (Gailmard 2014), but it does not provide Public Administration with a predictive theory for public accountability (Olsen 2013; Schillemans and Busuioc 2015). Rather, it offers an economic theory founded upon self-interest and fails to capture any concepts related to stewardship of public resources.

Many ground public accountability frameworks in the Friedrich-Finer debate of the 1940s but fail to look forward to where Arthur Maas and Laurence Radway outlined the types of accountability in their rarely cited article "Gauging Administrative Responsibility." Maas and Radway (1949) present their Simonian approach to moving away from principles of responsibility and moving toward a "criteria of responsibility" (p. 182). Their typology takes us to an end point similar to what we have reached in the past few decades: people-pressure groups, the legislature, the chief executive, the profession, and the courts. Forty years later, Romzek and Dubnick led us to a similar place; two decades thereafter, Bovens did the same. These well-established sources of accountability are helpful in diagnosing a problem, but a theoretical basis for public accountability remains underdeveloped.

Bovens (2010) suggests that we must examine accountability either as a "virtue" or as a "mechanism." "However," he says, "they should be differentiated from one another, since they each address different sorts of issues and imply very different sorts of standards, frameworks, and analytical dimensions" (p. 948). Mainly in attempts to create a parsimonious model, Bovens isolates accountability as a mechanism and relies on the idea of "forum", or "account holder," as central to the mechanical process. While he acknowledges that these two types of accountability are "complementary," he writes, "they should be clearly distinguished, as they address different kinds of issues and imply different standards and analytical dimensions" (p. 961). Accountability as a mechanism includes the following components:

1. There is a relationship between an actor and a forum
2. in which the actor is obliged
3. to explain and justify
4. their conduct,
5. the forum can pose questions,
6. pass judgment,
7. and the actor may face consequences.

O'Kelly and Dubnick (2014) offer a critical assessment of the Bovens model and highlight two chief concerns. First, they argue that the forum is overly reliant on the principal-agent model as a default framing. Second, they note that the Bovens model assumes "collective purpose" but offers very little in the development of that collective purpose (p. 10). O'Kelly and Dubnick (2014) write, "We see accountability as a far more pervasive matric of standpoints within which the individual negotiates their social existence, the group develops purpose and that purpose is normalised" (p. 10). The implication of their argument is that emergent relationships help to form accountability.

We concur with their assessment, also viewing emergent relationships as a key to an accountability theory. More specifically, the normative virtues of accountability establish expectations within the mechanism. If those expectations do not align with norms, then the mechanism itself will fail. Yet, there remains a theoretical void in the Public Administration related to public accountability. Only 26 percent of studies about accountability in Public Administration journals utilized an explicit theory in their paper, compared with 75 percent of Social Psychology studies (Schillemans 2013, p. 16).

Therefore, it is no surprise that in developing a theory of public accountability, some have considered Social Psychology literature (Busuioc and Lodge 2016; Schillemans 2016; Schillemans and Busuioc 2015). Busuioc and Lodge (2016) offer a perspective inspired by the work of Erving Goffman's *The Presentation of Self in Everyday Life* as an alternative to the P-A formulation. Based on a "reputational" approach, they develop predictions that are less reliant on formal structures of accountability. Rather, they provide a more flexible interpretation of how an actor can manage and shift based on maintaining their reputation and that of their organization. The predictions are as follows:

> We expect an emphasis on procedural appropriateness in the ways of doing things when it comes to activities that might be controversial in moral terms – and where professional and performative issues might be contested. An emphasis on moral aspects features where the overall performance cannot be observed in inputs, outputs, or outcomes. Technical elements, that is, the significance of a high level of professionalism, are emphasized when it is possible to point to the high degree of "ex ante" training and corps building that may then be used to discount a lack of evidence in terms of outputs or outcomes. Thus, reputation enhancement seeks to minimize controversy by emphasizing aspects that are difficult to dispute. (Busuioc and Lodge 2016, p. 250)

Busuioc and Lodge frame this article as providing a "competing theoretical" approach to the P-A model. Ultimately, they are "identifying reputation as a key variable in driving accountability behavior" (p. 3), thereby providing a theoretically relevant variable to consider – but they do not offer a theory upon which to build a series of hypotheses and tests. Schillemans and Busuioc (2015) made an alternative attempt. Rather than offering a clearly specified theory, they provide an initial step toward alternative postulations, making four major shifts from the P-A model and providing some potential avenues to pursue:

1. From Principal to Forum
2. From P_0 to P_2
3. From Agent to Steward
4. From Control to Legitimation

With each of these shifts comes a series of further considerations more pertinent to public accountability. First, one must consider the different types of forums; second, the timing and shifting of principals; third, the "intrinsic motivation" of the agent; and fourth, the "complex and reciprocal character of accountability processes in long-lasting professional relationships" (p. 211). Rooted in elements of public administration, this shift presents the actor as a steward of public goods, not one looking to enrich themselves. The implications of this model "would suggest not relying on mistrust-driven accountability requirements but to react to this problem by establishing trust" (Greiling and Spraul 2010, p. 354).

The Calibrated Public Accountability Model

Eventually, Schillemans (2016) offers the "Calibrated Public Accountability Model" or CPA-model. Leaning heavily on the Social Psychology literature, mainly the work of Philip Tetlock, Schillemans provides a working theory of public accountability. Schillemans lands on "three sets of independent variables, revolving around two aspects of the timing of accountability, two aspects relating to the relationship between the agent and his/her accountability forum and two aspects relating to the evaluative standards on the basis of which the agent is judged" (pp. 8–9). Schillemans (2016) notes, regarding the CPA-model, that "it is not designed to be the end point of the journey, but it is meant to be a starting point" (p. 1414). We take that cue and further refine the model and empirically test a set of related hypotheses. It is impossible to unhinge the CPA-model from its foundational elements developed in both Social Psychology and some sociological perspectives. Hence, we will use those elements to buttress the CPA-model as we develop testable hypotheses. In the following section, we will review Tetlock's contingency model and expand upon Schillemans's CPA-model.

According to Tetlock (1992), "Accountability is a critical rule and a norm enforcement mechanism – the social psychological link between individual decision-makers on the one hand and social systems on the other" (p. 337). It is what Lerner and Tetlock (1999a) call "a natural bridging construct between the individual and institutional level of analysis" (p. 256). We would take it one step further. Accountability is the connective tissue between the micro, meso, and macro levels of analysis. It is where societal values, institutional norms, and individual motivation collide, which is why modeling accountability presents such a challenge. Our lenses need to refocus as the concepts move from society to organization to individual and back again.

The contingency model upon which the CPA-model is built is based on four basic assumptions that are further developed into sub-propositions. The components are

1. the universality of accountability
2. the audience approval motive
3. motive competition
4. the linking of motive to coping strategies (Lerner and Tetlock 1999b)

First, Tetlock's contingency model proposes that the "universality of accountability" is nearly impossible to avoid (Lerner and Tetlock 1999b, p. 573). It assumes individuals have agency and are "capable of observing, commenting on, and controlling their own actions" (Tetlock 1992, p. 337). Furthermore, it assumes there are rules and norms, and that, shift as they may, individuals are tied to these broader rules and norms. As Dubnick (2002) explains, "What is distinctive about the accountability genre among other forms of governance solutions is its reliance on the existence of a 'moral community' that shapes (and is shaped by) the expectations, rules, norms and values of social relationships" (p. 6). Hence, if one were to deviate from the moral assumptions or the norms of the community, then they would have to justify their action – *they would be held accountable for their action* (Tetlock 1999). Accountability, then, is a constant reminder to people to "a) act in accord with prevailing norms; b) advance compelling justifications or excuses for conduct that deviates from those norms" (Tetlock 1999, p. 119).

This presumes accountability is dependent upon a broader value system, and that value systems may shift with place and time. These values help to establish the norms and customs that drive behavior and set the expectations *for what one is being held accountable*. Values differ based on the organizations and the organizations' broader connections to society, and those same values help to define the operational systems within an organization (Parsons 1956). This expectation supports the idea that we cannot isolate mechanisms from the virtues upon which they were built. Rather, the values provide context and legitimization to the mechanisms. Therefore, if public managers act as "stewards" of public resources working in organizations with "institutionalized values" (Schillemans and Busuioc, 2015, p. 209), then unlike their hypothesized behavior in the P-A model, they will voluntarily choose to disclose their actions (Schillemans and Busuioc 2015). Accountability, from this perspective, serves as "a way to build trust, credibility, and reputation" (Schillemans and Busuioc, 2015, p. 210), underscoring the second assumption of the contingency model – the audience approval motive. It proposes that people "seek the approval of the constituencies to whom they feel accountable" (Lerner and Tetlock, 1999b, p. 574). While public accountability theory may be able to rest on ideas of stewardship as a motivating factor, the contingency model provides flexibility for competing motivations in its third assumption, "motive competition" (Lerner and Tetlock 1999). The assumption is that there are multiple drivers of behavior. The fourth part of the contingency model – linking motive to coping strategies – is where one would observe individual/group accountability relationships, the step in which motives meet strategy. Hence, if my goal were to build trust with a forum, my behavior would look different then if my goal were to deceive a forum.

The CPA-model primarily makes propositions related to the fourth step in the contingency model. Schillemans lays out hypotheses for three dimensions: timing of accountability, the relationship between actor and forum, and the evaluative standard for accountability. Each dimension leads to set variables and related propositions that all predict how a manager would cope with an accountable relationship. Ultimately, if certain aspects are present, he proposes managers will make "accurate and well-considered decisions" that contrast with "inaccurate and un-reflected decisions" (Schillemans 2016, p. 1408).

Whereas the CPA-model provides the basis of the proposed theory, to advance the model we offer a slightly different perspective. First, we focus more broadly on the three dimensions of the model – timing of accountability, relationship with forum, and standards of evaluation. Within each of these dimensions, we offer further clarification and specification and do not rely on Schillemans's specification. Second, rather than using the terminology of "timing," we prefer *anticipated versus unanticipated accountability*. Last, rather than using the terminology "accurate and well-considered decisions," we use the terminology *multidimensional decisions*.

Dimensions of Accountability

Anticipated versus Unanticipated Accountability A recent empirical study comparing the felt accountability of thousands of local, regional, and national public servants in the Netherlands factored in anticipated accountability in the-development of a scale (Overman et al. 2020). Interestingly, their sample included police officers, who unlike other civil servants, view their account holder - the ministry of security and justice – as having a low level of expertise hence an illegitimate account holder(Overman et al. *forthcoming*, p. 14). Unlike Schillemans, we make no distinctions regarding the timing of accountability, seeing such distinctions as semantic rather than conceptual. Rather, we go directly to anticipated versus unanticipated accountability. If one knows they are going to be held accountable, then certain behaviors will follow. If one is unaware they will be held accountable, then different behaviors will arise. The CPA model proposes that someone who knows they are going to be held

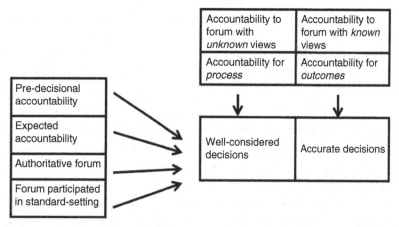

Figure 1 Calibrated Public Accountability Model

Source: Schillemans (2016, p. 1412)

accountable will make an accurate and well-considered decision. Following suit, our first proposition is that if one anticipates they are going to be held accountable, they will behave in a more multidimensional manner. If one does not anticipate being held accountable, they will defend the action taken.

Relationship between Forum and Actor The second dimension is the relationship between forum and actor. Schillemans identifies two variables: authoritative versus unauthoritative accountability forums and participating versus nonparticipating accountability forums. We endorse the broader dimension in the model; however, the distinction that Schillemans offers is not a clear alternative to the P-A model so we offer a modification.

The relationship between forum and actor might be the most important component of a theory of accountability. It presents an opportunity to step further away from the P-A model and lean on other drivers of exchange behavior. In their earlier work, Schillemans and Busuioc (2015) offer two concepts about the relationship between forum and actor – one of stewardship and one of legitimization. Stewardship implies that the actor is "intrinsically motivated" to behave in an accountable manner. Hence, they hypothesize that "If the actor is a highly trained professional or a professional organization, or when the actor has invested considerable time, assets and its reputation in a specific task and in developing expertise, it is more likely to apply itself to the task at hand and less likely to 'shirk'" (p. 209). Legitimization emerges as actors perform their tasks in accordance with established norms; rather than avoiding accountability, they encourage accountability (Schillemans and Busuioc 2015).

The ideas of legitimization and stewardship are fundamental to concepts about exchange and group dynamics, challenging the P-A model and providing an alternative explanation. These ideas assume actors have internalized the norms and do not need principals to constantly surveil their behavior to ensure compliance. This naturally occurs over time in group dynamics (Thibaut and Kelley 1959). At the root of these behaviors is how actors engage with one another. We are not the only scholars to make this jump. In an extensive theoretical review, Greiling et al. (2010) conclude: "From our point of view, social exchange theory might combine rational choice theory (embodied in principal-agent theory) with trust (stewardship theory) and ethical issues (critical accounting theory)" (p. 364).

Writing about exchange in the context of trading partners, Macneil (1986) offers the most direct alternative to the assumed P-A behavior. Macneil's work focuses on contractual relationships, which lends themselves well to the P-A model, but even in contractual relationships, we know that other factors must be considered. Central to Macneil's work is the concept of "social solidarity," which he uses interchangeably with trust. All exchange seeks to increase social solidarity. Similar to O'Kelly and Dubnick (2014), Macneil starts with basic exchanges like those that would occur in a bazaar. Individuals haggle with each other. They do so, according to Macneil, to understand the bounds of the trading relationship. Haggling allows trading partners to establish expectations and leads to exchanges in which both partners gain from the interaction. Haggling takes place in low-trust environs; however, through the iterative process, trust can be built. Hence, haggling with trusted friends is not necessary. The assumption is that friends will be looking out for your self-interest; trust is already established (Macneil 1986). Relationships vary on a spectrum of non-dependent individuals to interdependent, deep relationships. Macneil postulates that as interdependence grows, trust increases and is sustained. Macneil (1986) offers five steps in the process:

1. "Exchange requires sacrifice" on the part of both parties and will increase both "individual utility" and trust.
2. There is a balance between individual gains versus the increase of trust, which creates a tension and balance.
3. This tension demonstrates the complexities associated with human nature – driven by both self-serving and societal motives.
4. These inconsistencies are resolved by patterns of reciprocity.
5. The social processes appropriate to maintain or increase solidarity vary depending upon the level of solidarity already prevailing and the type of reciprocity being effectuated (p. 589).

The alternative approach laid out by Macneil provides a deeper understanding of how actors and forums might behave. This goes beyond Schillemans's postulations about forums. We argue that it is not the structure of the relationship that matters; rather, it is whether the actor and the forum have established social solidarity or trust. Hence, we propose that if the actor trusts the forum, then the actor will be more forthcoming with the forum about reporting their actions. If the forum is more trusting of the actor, it will grant the actor more discretion in disclosing their actions.

Standard for Evaluation The last component of Schillemans's model focuses on the standards for which one is held accountable. Broken down into two parts, this encompasses the "for what" question essential to the accountability formula. First, does the actor know the standards for which they are being held accountable, and second, does accountability focus on process or outcome? Schillemans (2016) proposes two paths, one geared toward "machine bureaucracies" that focuses on clear criteria and outcomes and one toward "professional organizations" that allows for flexibility in outcomes and process-oriented accountability (Schillemans 2016, p. 1412)

The simplicity of this dimension is quite elegant. Nevertheless, it needs further clarification. The most obvious criticism is what happens in situations of competing demands or multiple points of accountability. Operational systems in public organizations frequently have a combination of bureaucratic attributes and professional attributes inclusive of competing value systems with multiple sources of accountability. This characteristic has been given a good deal of attention in a series of articles about "hybrid organizations" by Christensen and Laegreid (2008, 2011, 2014). Christensen and Laegreid (2011) define "hybrid organizations" as "multifunctional entities combining different tasks, values and organizational forms. They are composite and compounded arrangements that are combining partly inconsistent considerations producing difficult and unstable trade-offs and lasting tensions" (p. 410). While one system might stress process-based accountability, a different system might stress outcome-based accountability.

We acknowledge these challenges and seek to build upon the CPA model. In this current project, we will not differentiate between organization types. Rather, we argue that components of both types of organizations must be accounted for. Therefore, we propose that if the evaluative criteria are clear and accountability is process oriented, then actors will make well-informed, multidimensional decisions. That said, we do not specifically test this dimension in the following empirical studies. Rather, we offer some insight into the expectations articulated by both US residents (the forum) and police chiefs (the actor) as to what is expected and what is delivered.

As Schillemans (2016) states,

> The CPA-model is designed as a tool that help us to navigate the interdisciplinary divide. It is not designed to be the end point of the journey, but it is meant to be a starting point – a collection of hypotheses, really – from which the external validity in "mundane reality" [Bozeman and Scott 1992, p. 309] of experimental findings can be explored and on the basis of which the impact of real-world intervening variables, such as politics, professional socialization or task-specificity, can be gauged. (p. 1414)

Ultimately, the CPA model offers an opportunity to test a predictive theory on accountability. While we make certain modifications, we endorse the three main dimensions within the model. Schillemans (2016) points researchers toward potential use of the model by noting one starting point is "to do experimental research with real-world participants" (p. 16). What has been missing, however, according to Han and Perry (2020, p. 298), is integration of a psychological approach into the accountability scholarship to foster the basis for a middle-range accountability theory of how public accountability systems shape individual decisions. This Element offers an opportunity to further build and test this model using just that – experimental research with real-world participants.

3 BWC Footage: When Police Chiefs Have Their Way

Introduction

Laws, policies, statutes, and directives about releasing video footage to the public show a high level of heterogeneity in the United States (Urban Institute 2018). Discretion occurs in the current environment as many police departments manage the flows of video footage captured by BWCs. In this section and in Section 4, we focus on two driving questions. First, what influences police chiefs' decisions about releasing footage to the public? Second, what do US residents expect in terms of accessing BWC footage of police-citizen interactions? Section 3 will focus on the first of those two questions. Driven by the Calibrated Public Accountability Model, we put forth multiple testable hypotheses in relation to accountability. Specifically, the research in this section focuses on the first two dimensions – anticipation of accountability and the relationship between actor and forum, focusing on transparency as the primary tool to achieve accountability. We view transparency, as does Roberts (2009), "as a mechanism of accountability; to cast light upon what would otherwise remain obscure or invisible, and to do so to provide the basis for confidence for distant others" (p. 957). We acknowledge that transparency alone is insufficient to achieve accountability; however, it tends to be a necessary component of an accountability system.

According to Chavis (2019), "The policies governing release of footage to the public have perhaps the greatest potential to impact community relations with the police" (p. 456). While we agree with the point Chavis makes, the current policy landscape defers much in relation to the power given to various police chiefs. Hence, we would rephrase the sentence and note that a *police chief's decision* to release "footage to the public will perhaps have the greatest potential to impact community relations with the police." Therefore, this research takes on the call from White and Malm (2020) to provide more research "into how departments provide the public with access to video footage" (p. 28). While it is generally presumed that the public should see these interactions captured by BWCs, the landscape of public disclosure is complex. As Maury (2016) notes, "The chance to observe a recording should not be confused with disclosure – the act of making something known to the public – which is a separate issue" (p. 499). Legally, chiefs may have to share footage with several other actors, but this does not require them to disclose footage publicly (Maury 2016).

This study focuses on that decision point – to share or not share footage of BWCs publicly. The "edit and share" decision is dubbed the fourth and final stage related to video surveillance by Hagen and colleagues (2018). They note that the decision breaks down into a series of decisions:

> Not only do decisions in this stage relate to what footage to release, but also to whom clips and associated data will be shared, when they are shared, how they are shared, and for what purpose. An organization might share clips with media. A lawyer might share clips with timestamps and locations with a jury. An employee might share clips with a coworker. Clips can be shared privately or broadcast to a wider audience. Decisions in this stage consider the intentions and goals of the entity in control of surveillance data. (Hagen et al. 2018, p. 282)

Hence, this decision point is a clear demonstration of to whom one thinks they are accountable and to whom one must use transparency as a tool to account for their actions.

Previous Research

Previous literature suggests several reasons that might affect a leader's decision to disclose video footage. This section draws on both law enforcement–specific literature and insight from the broader realm of Public Management literature. Research has primarily examined transparency as a precedent. Here, we ask what the antecedents of transparency are. What dictates one's willingness to share information with the public? Based on the CPA model, we consider two primary factors: anticipation of accountability and the relationship between the actor and the forum. We examine factors that may affect how the head of a law enforcement agency makes this decision in relation to the public disclosure of BWC footage, briefly addressing why timing may matter to accountability and then shifting to the matter of trust.

Anticipation of Transparency

Both the CPA model and the contingency model propose that known versus unknown accountability is a theoretically relevant factor. This primarily stems from Tetlock, Skitka, and Boettger (1989), who found that subjects went through more complex thought processes than unaccountable decision makers when they knew they would have to justify their decisions to an audience with unknown preferences. Alternatively, if a decision is made and confronted after the fact, the actor behaves in "defense bolstering" (Lerner and Tetlock 1999) – the process of defending actions regardless of complexity. These findings were supported in multiple experiments in relation to pilot safety and organizational accountability (Morris, Moore, Tamuz, and Tarrell, 1998) and with expressions of racial prejudice (Lambert, Cronen, Chasteen, and Lickel 1996). Research has consistently found that if one knows they will be held accountable prior to a decision, then they will engage in complex decision making, whereas if they do not know, they will robustly defend their original decision.

If one does not know they will be held accountable for their actions, then transparency will do little to achieve goals of accountability. Heald (2006) writes, "Timing of the introduction of transparency may have material impacts on the distribution of costs and benefits. Moreover, anticipation of these impacts may affect the behavior of those involved, sometimes in advance of the actual events" (p. 36). That would create scenarios that Fox (2007) identifies as "clear" transparency with "hard" accountability sanctions (p. 669). Ultimately, such scenarios should affect individual behavior. We derive one hypothesis that addresses the anticipation of the release of information.

H1 If a police chief can anticipate accountability, then they will behave in a more multidimensional manner in their decision making.

Thus, we would expect that if a police chief does not know or cannot anticipate they will be held accountable for an action, they will behave in a less complex manner in their decision making. They will participate in the process of defense bolstering.

The Relationship between Forum and Actor

Previous research has shown that police officers believe that BWCs will improve citizens' trust via transparency (White and Malm 2020, pp. 19–20). The examination of this topic has shown mixed results – with many studies pointing to the fallacy of this hypothesis (e.g., Tolbert and Mossberg 2006; Worthy 2010). O'Neill's poignant observation in her 2002 BBC Reith Lecture suggests that transparency is insufficient to achieve a trusting relationship:

> If we want to increase trust we need to avoid deception rather than secrecy. Although some ways of increasing transparency may indirectly reduce deception, many do not. Unless there has been prior deception, transparency does nothing to reduce deception; and even if there has been deception, openness is not a sure-fire remedy. Increasing transparency can produce a flood of unsorted information and misinformation that provides little but confusion unless it can be sorted and assessed. It may add to uncertainty rather than to trust. (O'Neill 2002)

However, transparency not leading to trust does not simply mean that transparency will not emerge in a trusting environment. In fact, in a high-trust environment, deception may disappear, and transparency may become a norm. In law enforcement, a trusting environment may be an essential component of effective policing. An overall high level of trust can enable a police agency "to thrive despite suffering the distrust of a significant minority of its population" (Worden and McLean 2017, p. 55). The importance of trust in policing and the pervasive belief that transparency will increase trust implies a more complex set of decisions in relation to releasing BWC footage to the public. We propose that factors of trust will be central to their decision points in scenarios where a chief determines the timing of a release of footage.

The relationship between citizens and administrators has always been an important consideration in Public Administration literature. Bartels (2013) recounts the history of this relationship and reminds readers that bureaucratic organizations are not founded upon a notion of close personal interactions. While a detailed historical account of this relationship is outside the scope of this section, the relationship itself is central.

The weight given to trust has led others to investigate the role it plays in administration, but few have examined public officials' trust in citizens. What appeared to be a promising avenue of research initiative by Yang (2005) has produced scant empirical evidence since then. Yang (2005) examined whether trust was relevant in engagement with citizens and found that trust is "a significant predictor of proactive implementation of citizen participation" (p. 282). Yang asserts, "Trust, unless otherwise proved, should become an ethical imperative for administrators and an institutional principle for system designers" (p. 282). Yang (2006) took this further to explore how trust in citizens affected their involvement in decision making, and concluded, "although trust is not always the solution, distrust is a problem. Democracy does not depend on trust, but too much distrust undermines democracy" (p. 591). Van de Walle and Lihi Lahat (2017) return to this framing while acknowledging the limited foundation. They test differences between levels of trust of public versus private officials and citizens, and the differences in an official's trust in citizens depending on political regime. There is little substantial difference between public and private officials, but differences are found based on political regime: "Trust among both public officials and non-public officials is much higher in social-democratic regimes, followed by corporatist countries and then liberal regimes" (p. 1460). Van de Walle and Lihi Lahat (2017) examine what leads to trust in public officials with the clear implication that heightened trust leads to several beneficial outcomes.

Law enforcement scholarship suffers from the same empirical chasm as does Public Administration. While there is extensive scholarship that asks, "Do citizens trust police?" there is limited research that asks the reverse. We have identified two studies that ask this question (Kääriäinen and Sirén 2012;

Mourtgos, Mayer, Wise, and O'Rourke 2020). Kääriäinen and Sirén (2012) ask, "Do the police trust in citizens?" Their study examines whether police officers in communities with higher levels of social capital experience higher levels of trust in their citizens. Their findings suggest this to be the case:

> Our findings suggest that police trust towards citizens can be explained with the very same factors that define generalized trust among citizens as a whole. Individuals who become police officers are born and raised and spend their adult lives in the same society with others. Our observations strongly indicate that the men and women working in the field of policing are, first and foremost, members of their respective communities. (Kääriäinen and Sirén 2012, p. 282)

Thus, these relationships are quite interrelated and are bound by the same features. Kääriäinen and Sirén (2012) suggest that, due to this "communal" perception, distrust may have wide implications for social justice and equity.

Expanding on this strain of research, Mourtgos, Mayer, Wise, and O'Rourke (2020) explore first what community attributes lead to an officer's trust in residents and second how does trust affect officers' performance. Their findings suggest "that police officers' trust in the public depends on their perception of the public's ability, benevolence, and integrity"(p. 661). Further, they found that officers who have higher levels of trust conduct more "proactive" police work leading to more arrests and potentially lowering crime rates (p. 661).

Outside of this work, there is minimal scholarship that directly addresses law enforcements' trust in citizens. However, this does lead to a connected line of research, albeit one that is equally limited, as to how media shapes police perceptions. In the age of BWCs, this point is especially relevant to perceptions of trust and the present section. Communal perceptions are shaped by many factors, and media may play a leading role. Nix and Pickett (2017) explore how officers perceive media coverage post-Ferguson. They examine whether officers think media coverage has any effect on crime and on perceptions of police officers, finding that more than 80 percent of the officers surveyed "believed that unfavorable media coverage of the police 'greatly increases' or 'increases' crime" (p. 30). Further, they find that officers believe that increased scrutiny by the media is having a significant impact on perceptions and feelings toward officers. Nix and Pickett (2017) write:

> Specifically, officers who believed media coverage of the police had been more hostile in recent years were significantly more likely to believe that civilians had become more distrustful, resentful, and disrespectful of police. Such officers were also more likely to report greater fear of being falsely accused of wrongdoing by civilians. In turn, officers' perceptions of civilians' attitudes toward police and fear of false accusations were both significantly related to their perceptions of crime trends. (p. 30)

The perception that media will sow seeds of distrust also emerges in data from a study conducted by Smykla, Crow, Crichlow, and Snyder (2016), who specifically asked how footage from BWCs would be used by the media. The authors report, "Almost 60 percent agree/strongly agree that the media will use data from BWCs to embarrass or persecute police and two-thirds (66.7 percent) agree/strongly agree that the use of BWCs is supported by the public because society does not trust police" (p. 438).

While we are limited in understanding the factors that affect an officer's trust in citizens, two questions naturally emerge. First, how does an officer's trust in citizens affect their behavior? Second, how does an officer's trust in the media affect their behavior? At best, the literature implies an officer may be more guarded; at worst, they will be completely closed off. For example, Adams and Mastracci (2019) explore well-being of officers in relation to the monitoring and distribution of BWC footage. They find, "As an officer perceives greater unfairness in the distribution procedures, and less caring for the impact on her well-being, she experiences greater intensity of monitoring" (p. 397). Trust is a concept that has received a great deal of attention. While we know much about one side of the relationship, we know very little about the other side – especially in relation to transparency. Transparency is a way in which to engage citizens in decision making; it provides them with information that they can use to make decisions.

Based on the CPA model and the concepts associated with trust, we propose two hypotheses:

H2 If police chiefs can anticipate accountability, then their level of trust in the residents in their community will influence their decision to release information.

H3 If police chiefs can anticipate accountability, then their level of trust in the media will influence their decision to release information.

Data and Methods

The survey was commented upon and pre-tested by one former police chief and one current police chief prior to being sent out. The sample was drawn from the National Public Safety Information Bureau (NPSIB) database of municipal law enforcement administrators. This database is accessible with a subscription fee. According to the NPSIB, the database includes "nearly every law enforcement agency in the nation." The list included email addresses for 12,586 police chiefs in the United States. Each case was assigned a random number and the list was split in half based on the random assignment. The survey was sent to 6,280 police chiefs and commanders (the first half of the list) with an email address. Of these, 413 of the email addresses were found to be erroneous or no longer valid. Of the 5,867 valid emails, 1,058 initial responses were received, for a response rate of 18 percent.

From these, we deleted the respondents who failed to properly answer the manipulation check question about the video vignette. We also discarded answers from respondents who took less than four minutes to complete the survey in the control group where only one video was presented, and those who took less than five minutes to complete the survey in the treatment group where two videos were presented. This is another way to ensure that the manipulation worked for respondents in the treatment group(s) (Mutz 2011, p. 88). Even before trimming the sample, the median duration of time to complete the survey was 1 minute and 23 seconds longer in the treatment group than in the control group. This makes us confident that the respondents in the treatment group watched that second one-minute video, which is our treatment.

At close to 84 percent, most of the respondents' titles are "Chief" or something comparable like "Interim Chief," and 14 percent are County Sheriffs. Less than 1 percent are running tribal law enforcement agencies. The typical department has 18 officers and protects 9,500 residents. The smallest departments in our sample have only one officer; the largest has 3,847. On average, chiefs or commanders oversee 52 officers and serve approximately 34,000 residents. Half the police forces in the United States have less than 10 full-time officers, and three-quarters have less than 25 (Friedman 2017, p. 315). Women comprise less than 3 percent of the surveyed chiefs or commanders; 4 percent preferred not to say, and the rest were males. The oldest chief was born in 1945, the youngest in 1998. The typical chief was 53 years old at the time of the survey. Roughly 3 percent of chiefs were African American, and less than 2 percent identified as American Indian or Alaska Native, Native Hawaiian, Pacific Islander, or Asian. Most of our respondents, 89 percent, described themselves as White.

Video Vignettes

Police chiefs were randomly assigned to two scenarios. Both video vignettes were similar in their story about a fatal encounter. However, the vignettes tried to represent, as organically as possible, a situation frequently dubbed a "dual recording," where citizens record the police for what they perceive to be self-protection and protest while officers record the interaction to meet "public demand for transparency, better evidence, and accountability" (Fan 2018b, p. 1647). In one scenario, a dual recording took place, while only a BWC captured footage in the other. This allowed us to manipulate the point at which a chief would be held accountable for the actions taking place in the footage.

To get to their true opinion and include chiefs from departments who do not currently have BWCs, the vignette frames the decision regarding whether or not to release video footage as advice requested by a police chief's friend. The idea was to copy the dynamics of local working groups and informal networks, through which many police chiefs trade policy snippets (White and Malm 2020, p. 78). To try to minimize police chiefs answering with their own policy, the scenario in the vignette mentions that the fatal encounter occurred during the pilot phase program, before the existence of a set BWC policy. The question is worth asking because police chiefs have significant leeway in how their departments are run: "When it comes to policing and its governance, our much-admired system of democratic accountability and transparency is largely cast aside. Policing agencies in the country – from your local police force to the Federal Bureau of Investigation – operate with very little democratic guidance" (Friedman 2017, p. 16). Table 1 shows the vignette's text and the layout of the experimental layout.

The motivation behind this choice permits testing of two propositions mentioned in the literature. First, the presence of a video "takes the narrative for a lethal or otherwise violent police-citizen encounter out of the control of police agencies and places it up for interpretation" (Graham et al. 2019, p. 297). Second, even for the police departments where the chief has plenty of discretion when it comes to sharing BWC footage, "the pressure of competing with a viral video gives law enforcement an incentive to expedite release" (Fan 2018b, p. 1675). However, this pressure also limits a chief's discretion in timing of release – the video is already public.

To minimize contagion from the details of one of the 1,000 real officer-involved police shootings happening every year in the United States, we used two 1-minute videos of the same scene filmed by police instructors at Quebec's National Police Academy located in Nicolet, QC, Canada. Videos 1 and 2 show three screenshots of the same moments, from the point of view of a smartphone and a police officer's BWC. No one was hurt or gunned down in the filming of these training videos.

Trust

For analytical purposes, we asked police chiefs to answer questions from two instruments: the "Trustworthiness items" and "Officer willingness to partner with the public items" for the police chiefs' "trust in citizens scale" (Carr and

Table 1 Experimental design for the survey experiment sent to police chiefs

	Control group (n/2)	Treatment group (n/2)
Text part of the vignette	We would like you to try your best to put yourself in this situation. Imagine, you recently received a phone call from a friend of yours who is a police chief in a nearby law enforcement agency. He asked you for advice in dealing with a recent incident concerning the footage captured from an officer's body-worn camera. His law enforcement agency is running a pilot program with body-worn cameras and the chief has yet to develop polices about the release of footage. Currently neither state laws, nor the collective bargaining agreement, address this issue so the chief is granted wide discretion in making this decision. He has turned to you as a close colleague and friend for guidance. Confidentially, he has shared with you the following video and asked if he should release it to the public. Law enforcement agencies across the country use a number of different practices.	Frame Treatment: We would like you to try your best to put yourself in this situation. Imagine, you recently received a phone call from a friend of yours who is a police chief in a nearby law enforcement agency. He asked you for advice in dealing with a recent incident concerning the footage captured from an officer's body-worn camera. His law enforcement agency is running a pilot program with body-worn cameras and the chief has yet to develop polices about the release of footage. Currently neither state laws, nor the collective bargaining agreement, address this issue so the chief is granted wide discretion in making this decision. He has turned to you as a close colleague and friend for guidance. Confidentially, he has shared with you the following videos and asked if he should release it to the public. The first video was captured by the cell phone of a bystander close to the

	Some agencies release videos immediately while others prefer to edit the videos prior to release.	incident. It is circulating online and being shown by local media outlets. The second video was captured by the officer's body-worn camera. Law enforcement agencies across the country use a number of different practices. Some agencies release videos immediately while others prefer to edit the videos prior to release.
Video part of the vignette	Fatal encounter filmed by BWC (see images x)	Fatal encounter filmed by BWC (see images x) Fatal encounter filmed by a smartphone (see images c)

Video 1 Three screenshots of the training video depicting a fatal encounter filmed by a smartphone. Video available at www.cambridge.org/bromberg

Video 2 Three screenshots of the training video depicting a fatal encounter filmed by an officer's BWC. Video available at www.cambridge.org/bromberg

Maxwell 2018) and the sixteen-item "Trust in News Media" scale (Kohring and Matthes 2007). Tables 2 and 3 show the descriptive statistics for the instruments and their constitutive items.

Results

When asked to suggest to their police chief friend the way forward after an officer-involved fatal shooting, 48.7 percent of respondents suggested waiting to release the raw footage until after the internal investigation. The other options were significantly less popular: 26.8 percent favored a narrated version, 12.5 percent recommended not releasing the footage, and only 12.2 percent recommended releasing the raw footage of the encounter immediately (see Table 4). Many police chiefs added in a free-text box that the reason why the footage should not be released is that the resident killed by police showed obvious signs of mental illness.

Table 2 Chiefs' trust in their residents

Statements	n	mean	SD	Min	Max
The people in the community we serve approach life with a strong moral code.	708	5.57	0.91	2	7
The people in the community we serve care about what happens to police officers.	708	5.95	0.87	1	7
The people in the community we serve are capable of "policing" themselves.	707	4.05	1.43	1	7
I would be comfortable giving a person in the community we serve a task that is important, even if I could not monitor his/her actions.	708	4.66	1.32	1	7
If I had my way, I would let the people in the community we serve have an influence over issues that are important to me.	705	4.26	1.38	1	7
If I had my way, I would let the people in the community we serve have a say in how the department conducts policing activities in their neighborhood.	707	4.51	1.45	1	7
Chiefs' Trust in Residents	**708**	**4.83**	**0.84**	**3.8**	**7**

Adapted from Carr and Maxwell's (2018) "Trustworthiness items" and "Officer willingness to partner with the public items"; Cronbach alpha 0.99

Table 3 Chiefs' trust in the news media

Statements	n	mean	SD	Min	Max
The topic of law enforcement receives the necessary attention.	707	4.88	1.37	1	7
The topic of law enforcement is assigned an adequate status.	705	4.75	1.38	1	7
The frequency with which law enforcement is covered is adequate.	706	4.86	1.38	1	7
The topic of law enforcement is covered on the necessary regular basis.	707	4.86	1.34	1	7
Selectivity of topics Cronbach alpha 0.99	707	4.84	1.28	1	7
The essential points of law enforcement activities are included.	706	4.38	1.49	1	7
The focus is on important facts concerning law enforcement activities.	705	4.27	1.49	1	7
All important information regarding the topic of law enforcement is provided.	705	3.90	1.54	1	7
Reporting includes different points of view.	706	4.13	1.60	1	7
Selectivity of facts Cronbach alpha 0.99	707	4.17	1.38	1	7
The information in a report would be verifiable if examined.	704	4.74	1.42	1	7
The reported information is true.	702	4.60	1.45	1	7
The reports recount the facts truthfully.	704	4.56	1.51	1	7
The facts that I receive regarding law enforcement activities are correct.	703	4.71	1.40	1	7
Accuracy of depictions Cronbach alpha 0.97	706	4.66	1.32	1	7
Criticism is expressed in an adequate manner.	701	4.35	1.50	1	7
The journalists' opinions are well founded.	703	3.85	1.50	1	7
The commentary regarding law enforcement activities consists of well-reflected conclusions.	700	3.92	1.52	1	7

Table 3 (cont.)

Statements	n	mean	SD	Min	Max
I feel that the journalistic assessments regarding the topic of law enforcement are useful.	705	4.16	1.58	1	7
Journalistic assessment Cronbach alpha 0.97	705	4.07	1.38	1	7
Chiefs' Trust in the News Media	**683**	**4.43**	**1.20**	**1**	**7**

Adapted from Kohring and Matthes's (2007) Trust in News Media scale.

Table 4 Distribution for answer to this question: "What would you most likely suggest your colleague do with the video footage?"

	Police chiefs
The police department should not release the footage.	12.5% (87)
The police department should release the raw footage of the encounter once an internal investigation is over.	48.7% (427)
The police department should release a narrated version of the footage of the encounter so the public understands police procedures.	26.8% (182)
The police department should immediately release the raw footage of the encounter.	12.2% (85)

Even with four options, close to a majority of police chiefs recommended that their friend, who did not have a clear BWC policy, wait to release the BWC footage until `after an internal investigation. Figure 2 illustrates the differences in recommendations about the timing of BWC footage release, among police chiefs assigned to the control group, where the BWC version is the only one that exists, and the treatment group, where a version of the incident captured on a smartphone is already circulating on social media.

Comparisons of means across the control and the treatment groups do not reveal statistically significant differences between groups (Pearson $chi^2(3)$ = 2.8330, Pr = n.s.; t = 0.30, Pr = n.s.; β=-0.004, std err.= 0.071). Overall, the police chiefs are not swayed one way or another with their recommendation, just by our treatment – at least, not in proportions large enough to be

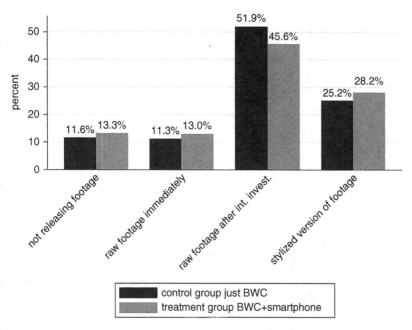

Figure 2 Suggestion for "What would you most likely suggest your colleague do with the video footage?" by experimental conditions

statistically significant with our sample size of 699 police chiefs. That lack of large differences between conditions speaks to shared professional values among police chiefs.

The next question is to determine how different kinds of trust – trust in citizens and trust in the media – can shape the recommendations of police chiefs. Table 5 shows the results of how the two kinds of trust correlate with the BWC footage release suggestions. We ran separate models for police chiefs in the control and treatment groups.

To ease comprehension, we did not report small coefficients and large standard errors. Researchers who would like to obtain them for replication of meta-analysis purposes can contact the authors.

For police chiefs in the scenario where BWC footage is the only existing video recording, the relative probability of suggesting chiefs not release the BWC footage, rather than release the raw footage immediately, is 48.9 percent lower for police chiefs with higher trust in their citizens. The relative probability of releasing raw footage after internal investigation rather than releasing raw footage immediately is also 39 percent higher for police chiefs with higher trust in the media than for chiefs with lower trust.

Table 5 Results of multinomial regression of police trust in citizens and trust in the media, by the existence of smartphone footage of a fatal encounter, with releasing raw footage immediately as the base outcome

Suggestion for footage release	Variables	Participants with fatal encounter filmed by BWC % odds ratio (std. err)	Participants with fatal encounter filmed by BWC + smartphone % odds ratio (std. err)
not releasing footage	Trust in citizens	- 48.9%*	n.s.
		(0.33)	(n.s.)
vs.	Trust in media	n.s.	n.s.
releasing raw footage immediately		(n.s.)	(n.s.)
releasing raw footage after internal investigation	Trust in citizens	n.s.	n.s.
		(n.s.)	(n.s.)
vs.	Trust in media	39.0%*	n.s.
releasing raw footage immediately		(0.16)	(n.s.)
releasing stylized version of footage	Trust in citizens	n.s.	n.s.
		(n.s.)	(n.s.)
vs	Trust in media	n.s.	n.s.
releasing raw footage immediately		(n.s.)	(n.s.)
		n=336	n=358
Nagelkerke R2		0.06	0.03

For police chiefs in the scenario where smartphone footage is circulating online and shown by local media outlets, variations of trusts in their communities and the media do not influence suggestions to release BWC footage.

Discussion

BWCs have many upsides. Reviewing the empirical literature, Ariel (2019) recalls that BWCs improved policing where training, external reviews, and department guidelines failed (p. 499). That is not to say that accountability is heightened with the mere use of BWCs in a police force. McElroy (2019b) mentions the following:

> Some in law enforcement would argue that the whims of people on social media shouldn't impact their decision making process. Yet the reality is that social media has changed the way people live, communicate, and conduct business. Social media has become the number-one activity on the Web.

Our results show that social media will not affect a police chief's decision to release a video. There was no statistical difference between the condition of a video circulating on social media and one not circulating. Overall, nearly 50 percent of all chiefs would prefer to release the video after an internal investigation. The least favored option was to release footage right away. There are two scenarios where we examine how a chief, sheriff, or leader of a law enforcement agency discloses the footage of a BWC. In one scenario, the chief has limited ability to control disclosure. Smartphone footage has already been circulating. In the second scenario, the chief has complete discretion and the ability to control disclosure. In the scenario with a smartphone, the chief's variation of trust in different groups makes no significant difference in their suggestion to release BWC footage. Those with high levels of trust and those with low levels of trust behave in the exact same manner. In scenario two, trust does matter.

In scenario one, the release of the BWC footage offers little new information. Hence, a chief is given a series of options, but each adds marginal information. The options in scenario one seems to exist in a chief's "zone of indifference" (Barnard 1968, p. 169). It is in this zone in which it seems that the chiefs' levels of trust do not change behavior. In scenario two, a chief is in full control of the disclosure of information. Movement from sharing raw footage of a video to sharing the video with some constraints is dramatically modified by a chief's varying levels of trust. The most substantial shift occurs when a chief has higher levels of trust in their own community. A chief's willingness to share BWC footage when community trust is higher increases dramatically. This finding suggests that a leader is willing to share information with the public if they trust the forum with whom they are sharing. One limitation to our video vignette is that the subject that is depicted is a middle-aged white man.

Conclusion

The contributions of this study are twofold. First, there is a gaping hole in the literature regarding the examination of public officials' trust in citizens. Second, this study moves the theory of public accountability forward by demonstrating support for components of the CPA model. Primarily, we find that when police chiefs are in control of the timing of the release of footage, meaning they can anticipate exactly when they will be held accountable for an action, they will make a more complex decision. Furthermore, we identify trust as a component of that complex decision-making process. In scenarios where chiefs have no way to anticipate when they will be held accountable, trust is no longer a factor in the decision-making process.

As White and Malm (2020, p. 19) recognize, some police departments decrease transparency by creating many restrictions to public access to BWC footage. Our results fit with Friedman's (2017) assertion that "public attention is the lever that can pry loose many a stuck rock. Once the public cares, and the media is engaged, then legislators no longer can avoid the issue: they are forced to take positions, to listen, and perhaps to act" (p. 102). However, the CPA model predicts, and our study confirms, that both the timing of accountability and the relationship between actor and forum will lead to more complex behavior when the actor is held to account.

4 BWC Footage: "What Do We Want? When Do We Want It?"

Introduction

Little is known about local preferences regarding BWCs and the release of video footage. As an electoral issue, BWC use does not score high. As one officer recounted, "*No one* attended scheduled meetings on July 11 and on Wednesday at which the Winchester Police Department planned to show residents how the cameras work and brief them on the camera policy, which also includes privacy issues" (Goodenow 2018). While it is assumed that small police and sheriff departments could be more in touch with the needs of the communities they serve and have a better sense of their residents' preferences in relation to BWCs (J. Smith 2019, p. 380), little empirical evidence supports this notion.

Ultimately, this disconnect leads to wide policy variation and rules that might have similar intent being implemented in different manners across jurisdictions. For example, Oakland, California, and Houston, Texas, have attempted to limit disclosure of footage that reveals personal information contained on a driver's license or insurance card. Oakland's Police Department will simply not release a video with this content; Houston's, on the other hand, will release footage but redact that information (Pagliarella 2016, p. 538). This variation leads to other policy differentiations. To balance the heightened cost of redacting videos, the Houston Police Department stores videos for a shorter period, saving money on storage costs (Pagliarella 2016, p. 538).

There are also situations in which authority falls under multiple jurisdictions. Therefore, while the entity that represents local preferences might have some control, a different entity may have final decision-making power. For example, the state of California and the Port of Seattle Commission have banned the use of facial recognition software in various surveillance technologies. This, in theory, represents local preferences. However, LAX was the first American airport to have facial-only biometric boarding (Reynolds 2019), and Seattle-Tacoma International Airport, run by the Port of Seattle Commission, has engaged facial-recognition—enabled cameras to process international travelers (www.portseattle.org/facialrecognition). Both airports fall within the jurisdiction of multiple entities, and the federal government controls these aspects – allowing for the technology to prevail. This misalignment between local preferences and federal requirements presents a challenge.

That said, many scholars still believe that the implementation of BWCs provides residents with the accountability they want. As Chavis (2019) notes, BWC footage offers an objective account of an incident, making accountability possible (p. 453). Braga, Brunson, and Drakulich (2019) include BWCs along with other proven strategies to bolster better relationships between communities with low levels of trust for the police and police departments (p. 549). However, they are quick to point out that the "adoption of body-worn cameras should be accompanied by police department policies that facilitate the appropriate public viewing of captured video footage to generate the desired enhancements to transparency and police accountability" (Braga, Brunson, and Drakulich 2019, p. 549). These scholars' lofty hopes for BWCs are possible, but each of their conclusions is loaded with complexity; they assume we understand what will lead to accountability and what citizen preferences are for these policies. This section clarifies the expectations of US residents' policy preferences, which can lead to a joint set of accountability expectations and policy preferences. This is a key aspect of the CPA model. If one knows the expectations to which they will be held to account, they will make well-considered decisions. Thus far, specific public preferences have remained obscured.

Previous Research

The public at large is supportive of BWCs. Summarizing seven studies for the use of BWCs in 2016 and 2017, Graham and colleagues (2019, p. 287) report a range of support from 76 percent to 92 percent. In a more recent study of more than 3,000 Americans, regarding citizen support of BWCs, Miethe and colleagues (2019, p. 272) find an overall support level of 83 percent for "all areas of police work," with levels as high as 90 percent and 89 percent for crime scene investigation and crowd control, respectively. Respondents seeing procedural fairness positively in their police department show strong support for BWCs, which does not appear to be affected by demographic, geographic, or income criteria (Graham et al., 2019; Miethe et al. 2019). However, it is possible that a consensus exists about certain elements of BWC policies, but the details of those policies are where we might find discrepancies.

In 2018, the Policing Project, a research group directed by Barry Friedman, organized a public consultation of citizens and police officers in Los Angeles. Aside from two petitions and briefs received by twenty-seven organizations, 3,199 surveys were filed by individuals studying, working, or residing in Los Angeles, including 532 self-identifying law enforcement officials (Policing Project 2018a, p. 1). Many of the questions in the survey had to do with preferences about releasing BWC footage. Quick release of footage was seen as more transparent than tardier release: "Indeed, of the 67% of public respondents who said that video should 'definitely' be made public at some point, the vast majority said that release should happen quickly: 64% said within 30 days, and another 18% said within 60 days" (Policing Project 2018a, p. 14). When asked how much they would trust different officials to share BWC footage on a case-by-case level, only 35 percent of Angelinos would trust their chief of police in general, and only 12 percent would trust them a great deal (Policing Project 2018a, p. 26). A similar but larger civic consultation in New York City revealed that when asked when the NYPD should release footage of high-profile incidents, 51 percent of respondents said "as soon as possible," 25 percent said "after an internal investigation," and 17 percent said "at the end of any court case or judicial proceeding" (Policing Project 2018b, p. 29). Only 3 percent said "never," and 5 percent did not have an opinion (Policing Project 2018b, p. 29). In an interview, David McNeil, chief of the Aberdeen Police Department in South Dakota, mentioned that quickly sharing BWC footage with the public serves the department's interests: "[Agencies are] using it to mitigate riots and protests and that sort of thing in the community" (Miller 2019).

While citizens generally want to see footage, a range of questions remains. For example, in 2014, a citizen of Washington State requested "all footage from every officer in the Seattle Police Department" (Gaub et al. 2017, p. 10). The cost to process such a request is prohibitive. Other policies, such as that of Charlotte-Mecklenburg's Police Department, require a court order to obtain footage. As Alpert and McLean (2018) note, "Although no studies have been aimed at examining whether this requirement is seen as positive or negative by community members and other stakeholders, it is unlikely that making BWC footage harder to access will make departments seem more transparent" (p. 4). While there is progress toward understanding the demands of residents, our understanding remains underdeveloped. As Uchida, Haas, and Solomon (2019) suggest regarding the LAPD release policy, careful empirical studies are needed to further our understanding of privacy and accountability preferences.

Reasons Why BWC Footage Is Not Available

While demands for BWC use have grown substantially, and expectations for the release of footage remain constant, a law enforcement agency may not release footage for many reasons. As this study remains focused on that decision point, we will briefly review reasons behind not releasing footage.

Failure of Camera to Activate Many reasons can explain why an officer did not activate a BWC to film an incident. Lawrence and colleagues (2019, p. 341) suggest three explanations: the officer forgot, the officer intentionally did not activate their camera, or the officer did not have time to activate their camera. As one district attorney from Berks County, Pennsylvania, observed: "We have had situations where the officer did not turn his body camera on. . . . It is always subject to human error. That is a problem" (Long 2020). Ariel (2019) reminds us that assuming perfect execution of implementation of a policy in a hierarchical and para-militaristic organization like a police force is a mistake; officers will and do resist innovations and reforms (p. 494). Some will turn their BWC on or off selectively (Franks 2017, p. 35).

If Graham and colleagues (2019, p. 288) are correct that "the use of BWCs appears to be a crucial step in meeting community expectations of police transparency and accountability," the failure to activate a camera may have consequential effects. As Lawrence and colleagues (2019) suggest, "if an officer's failure to activate his or her BWC comes to the attention of the public, this could actually negatively impact efforts to demonstrate transparency and generate community trust" (p. 341). That impact can be dire. All of the efforts through "months or years of building community trust can be wiped out by one failure to activate in a critical incident" (White and Malm 2020, p. 105).

Camera malfunctions also happen. A 2019 study out of Baltimore found 8 percent of their police CCTV cameras to be inoperative (Rector 2019). In 2018, one BWC in New York City caught fire. Systematic BWC malfunctions have happened in the Toronto Police Service (Canadian Broadcasting Company 2017). Some authors, like Graham and colleagues (2019, p. 297), suspect that a BWC malfunction during an incident could undermine police objectivity in the eyes of citizens. Hence, regardless of *why* a camera is not turned on, law enforcement will face scrutiny.

Mental Health In a systematic review "performed with seven multidisciplinary databases," Livingston (2016) identified hundreds of thousands of interactions between the police and those living with mental illness. Livingston estimates that 25 percent of those living with mental illness have been arrested by the police, 12 percent of those living with mental illness have been directed to mental health services by the police, and about 1 percent of all police dispatches involve interactions with a person with mental illness. According to the *Washington Post*'s "Fatal Force" Database, about 22 percent of the people killed by police using fatal force suffered from mental illness. These interactions between those suffering from mental illness and law enforcement range in scope, but one can understand how a BWC may introduce a challenging element. In certain situations, a camera can escalate behaviors; in other situations, privacy concerns may arise (Taylor 2016). In 2015, a judge in New Hampshire ruled in favor of disclosing footage after the family of a man suffering from mental illness requested the footage not be made public (Rodgers 2015). The judge ordered certain parts of the video be redacted, but such a ruling could run counter to citizens' expectations of full disclosure.

Bromberg, Charbonneau, and Smith (2018) showed that New Hampshire residents underreport their desire to see footage from BWCs, including footage of those suffering from mental illness. Upward of 66 percent supported viewing this type of footage, whereas in a broader sample of US residents, 86 percent supported viewing this footage. This is a challenging line for both legal experts and law enforcement to draw. Should footage be made public if a victim or perpetrator suffers from mental illness?

Internal Investigation Internal investigations may prohibit immediate release of video footage for several reasons. First, prior to releasing footage, law enforcement and legal teams must ensure a video does not violate privacy laws. According to Maury (2016), this may include

> the death of a person not caused by law enforcement, identifying minors under sixteen years of age, identifying victims of sex crimes or domestic

abuse, witnesses providing information to law enforcement, confidential informants, information that would "materially" compromise an ongoing law enforcement investigation, and identities of officers subject to internal investigation. (p. 510)

Second, if prosecutors in legal proceedings use video evidence, there are other concerns. A fear exists that a "trial by media" will take place, rather than one in the courthouse (Uchida, Hass, and Solomon 2019). A journalistic investigation of officer-involved shootings examined the availability of video footage after the 105 incidents in 2017. In early 2018, footage for 40 cases was tracked (Bogen 2018). Some states, like Texas, prohibit video release until investigations are completed; Bogen (2018) comments that "police chiefs and district attorneys frequently postpone release, claiming that making video public would undermine the integrity of an investigation or taint a jury pool" (Bogen 2018).

Reasons for releasing or not releasing footage vary. The three identified earlier are some of the most prominent in the BWC literature and policy implementation. Our research design accounts for these three policy scenarios.

Trust

As noted in our theoretical section, we identify trust as a key variable in the relationship between the actor and the forum. In Section 2, our model incorporates a police chief's trust in their community as a determinant for releasing video footage. As trust is a relational concept, it is equally important to determine how a resident's level of trust in police affects their perspective of policing. In their rich and multipronged analyses of two police departments in New York State, including follow-up citizen surveys of police interactions, some of them filmed and analyzed by the researchers, Worden and McClean (2017) conclude the following:

> In view of previous research, we have compelling reason to suppose that the omission of citizens' prior attitudes from these models leaves them misspecified; prior attitudes toward the police generally have a strong effect on subjective procedural justice. Thus we added our measure of legitimacy – the trust index – to the model in order to gauge the extent to which the estimated relationships are biased by the omission of prior attitudes. (p. 142)

The researchers go even further regarding the limits of observed procedural justice in civilian-police encounters to influence trust in the police, emphasizing that citizen satisfaction after an encounter is not only subjective but much more subjective than previously thought (Worden and McClean 2017, p. 185), and they even comment that surveys of recent interactions might be of limited utility (Worden and McClean 2017, p. 186):

Given the weak connections between what officers do (and do not do) and what citizens later think about it, we might well see little or no change in survey-based measures of performance with good faith – even herculean – efforts by platoon commanders and field supervisors to manage their officers' behavior in police-citizen encounters. (Worden and McClean 2017, p. 180)

That conclusion, compounded with negativity bias, underlines the destructive effects of rare fatal shootings of civilians by police officers. Officers can be courteous and professional for a long time, without improving a community's trust in the police, and one tragic accident can erode police trust for a long time. How police chiefs decide to handle the release of BWC footage to the public can further damage this trust.

Accountability is complex, and knowing the standards upon which one is evaluated is an essential component (Schillemans 2016). Therefore, we will gain an understanding of those standards by knowing citizens' preferences for BWC access. We will also compare differences across three cities, frequently referenced as three divergent policy models in the literature, and across residents of the United States at large.

Data and Methods

Previous studies of citizens' assessment of BWC video vignettes have suffered from small sample sizes and unreliable or dubious sources of sampling, making otherwise interesting designed studies' results suspect (Hamm et al. 2019; Turner at al. 2019). In this section, we use video vignettes with four large samples of citizens. By design, for each sample, 40 percent of respondents were shown the BWC version of the incident and an additional text component of the vignette. That is the treatment. We expect that respondents randomly assigned to that condition will agree with the chief's handling of the BWC footage more than the three control conditions. Further, we expect they will rate the police department's level of transparency in disclosing information about this incident as more transparent than the three control conditions where respondents cannot see the interaction.

Respondents read the description of the incident; they were told to put themselves in the scenario. The part of the description that was common across all experimental conditions was as followed:

Release: We would like you to try your best to put yourself in this situation. Imagine there was a recent incident in your community in which an officer used deadly force after a traffic stop. The Chief of Police held a press conference to provide preliminary information. The Chief stated, "At approximately 2:35 PM two officers approached a car that was pulled over on the side of the road. There was a Caucasian male inside the car behaving erratically. The officer knocked on the car window but received no response. At approximately 2:36PM the male stepped outside of the car and banged his fists on the roof of the vehicle. He remained unresponsive to the officer. The male then reached into his vehicle and pulled out a large ax and began approaching the officers swinging the ax in their direction."

The remaining 60 percent of the respondents were not given the video footage. Rather, they were only given a text vignette with one of three reasons why the fatal incident was not filmed by the BWC. The reason given to 20 percent of the respondents was "The officer failed to activate his camera; therefore, we are unable to release any footage from the scene of the incident." The reason given to another 20 percent of respondents was as follows:

> The officer was wearing a body-worn camera at the time of the incident; however, the family of the perpetrator has requested that we keep the footage private because the individual suffered from mental illness. We are honoring this request and currently not releasing the body-worn camera footage to the public.

The reason given to the final 20 percent of the sample was "We are currently conducting an internal investigation of the incident. Once the investigation is complete, we will make a determination about the release of the body-worn camera footage."

We used four samples of 1,000 residents for this survey: the United States at large, plus three metropolitan areas. Luc.Id, a survey firm based in New Orleans, Louisiana, recruited respondents from web panels. The sample of Americans was meant to reflect the United States as a whole on sociodemographic characteristics. The other three samples were not. However, we later calculated weights to better reflect the sociodemographic characteristics of the three cities. However, the results varied little between results stemming from the weighted and unweighted responses. In the academic and practitioner literature, three cities are mentioned repeatedly as divergent models for BWC public release of footage policies: Charlotte, North Carolina; Seattle, Washington; and Los Angeles, California:

> In Washington State, where public records laws are liberal, the Seattle Police Department responded to a wave of public records requests by exacting nearly all footage and uploading it to a public YouTube channel. ... In 2016, for example, the North Carolina General Assembly passed House Bill 972, which classified BWC and dashboard-camera footage as part of officers' personnel records, and a court order is now required before BWC footage can be released. ... The LAPD recently implemented a forty-five-day release policy for critical incidents, such as officer-involved shootings. The Seattle Police Department policy manual states that within seventy-two hours

of an officer-involved shooting, the department will release a "representative and relevant sample" of available video. (White and Malm 2020, p.112)

The United States The Fourth Amendment of the US Constitution limits use of force by the police. If an officer uses a reasonable level of force, the police department has no civil or criminal liability (Chavis 2019, p. 454). For the current study, the sample of US residents at large works as a baseline to which cities can be compared. A total of 1,053 respondents are in the group.

Charlotte, North Carolina The Charlotte-Mecklenburg Police Department was deemed a department where supervisors applied strict restrictive policies for the use of force (Terrill and Paoline 2017, p. 213). In 2015, the North Carolina state legislature mandated the use of police BWCs (White and Malm 2020, p. 96). A full law review article testified to the opacity of the public release clauses of BWC footage in North Carolina (Liebman 2015). Departments in this state are not required to release footage (p. 368), "and no court in North Carolina is likely to force the issue" (p. 368). Under North Carolina's public records law, "all body camera footage, be it of a police shooting, the inside of someone's home, or of a rape victim, will fall within one nontransparent bucket: records of criminal investigations" (p. 368). This public footage release policy has been qualified as troubling since a court order is needed to share data "even in cases where police agencies want to make the footage public" (Bogen 2018). In a 2019 interview, a spokeswoman for the American Civil Liberties Union of North Carolina commented that video surveillance was becoming more widespread, even in smaller towns in North Carolina, that checks and balances were lacking, and that North Carolinians did not trust that cities were taking action with the acquired footage (Barrett 2019).

The 2016 North Carolina law is presented as an example of "countertransparency body-camera laws," which are emulated by other states like South Carolina, Louisiana, and Kansas (Stroud 2019, p. 209). We have a total of 998 participants from the Charlotte metro area.

Los Angeles, California Los Angeles has been an early adopter of police tactics such as SWAT teams (Turner and Fox 2019, p. 123) and police technologies, including facial recognition software added to BWCs (Garvie and Moy 2019) and a gang database (Judd 2019). The LAPD started deploying BWCs in 20015 (McCluskey et al. 2019 p. 214). Los Angeles seeks regular public input via its board of commissioners, which ends up shaping their policing policies (Friedman 2017, p. 17). In 2018, the LAPD was collecting 14,000 BWC recordings per day and had accumulated more than 2 million hours of footage (Puente 2018).

At times compared disparagingly with Seattle, the LAPD set a low bar that became a legislated minimum in the state of California, where all local law enforcement agencies must release officer-shooting BWC footage within forty-five days. Famously, the LAPD offers a "a well-produced community briefing that is released on its YouTube channel within 45 days of an officer-involved shooting" (McElroy 2019a). This briefing includes "raw BWC footage, narration, and commentary from department officials" (White and Malm 2020, p. 112). The Board of Police Commissioners, which includes civilian members, worked to design this policy and set the exceptions (Uchida, Hass, and Solomon 2019). These video briefings have been described as "thorough and informative" but also as "too edited and orchestrated" (McElroy 2019a). A total of 1,023 Angelinos participated in this study.

Seattle, Washington Seattle is one of the many cities where the murder rate fell by at least half between the 1990s and the 2010s (Sharkey 2018, p. 26). A 2016 law review article chronicled that due to the high cost to manually redact video footage as well as respect and comply with one citizen's disclosure request, the Seattle Police Department (SPD) almost eliminated its entire BWC program; only a compromise with that citizen averted that decision (Pagliarella 2016, p. 558). This was a reflection of the state-level policies. In the early 2010s, a state court forced the Seattle Police Department to release video surveillance footage after a news station sued the city of Seattle (Newell 2014, p. 426). Since that period of opacity, SPD has been touted as an example of transparency in academic writings and the news media. Seattle is one of the few cities, along with Chicago, where their policing manual can be consulted by the public on the Internet (Friedman 2017, p. 17).

In Seattle, many pieces of police information are released within twenty-four hours, including all BWC footage as well as "related surveillance video, photographs of a subject's weapons, and a basic statement providing the initial facts of the case" (McElroy 2019). At press conferences, raw footage is shared and police officials answer questions and explain the related chain of events (White and Malm 2020, p. 112). That twenty-four-hour release practice is self-imposed, as the SPD's policy is to release information within seventy-two hours (McElroy 2019). A total of 1,007 respondents from Seattle participated in this study. Table 6 presents sociodemographic information about the participants of the four groups.

Results

Respondents in the three cities and in the United States at large answered three main questions after being shown, or not, the video of the fatal shooting. The footage, pictured in Figure 3, is the same BWC footage showed to police chiefs in Section 2.

Table 6 Basic sociodemographic information about the participants, before weighting

Sociodemographic		United States	Seattle, WA	Los Angeles, CA	Charlotte, NC
Age	18–34	33.6% (354)	34.0% (343)	31.3% (320)	36.0% (333)
	35–54	28.6% (301)	31.5% (317)	36.6% (373)	36.1% (334)
	55+	27.8% (293)	26.0% (262)	24.9% (255)	25.9% (258)
	(missing)	10.0% (105)	8.4% (85)	7.2% (75)	7.3% (73)
Gender	male	34.8% (366)	47.4% (477)	42.2% (432)	46.4% (463)
	female	54.3% (572)	43.9% (442)	49.5% (506)	45.5% (454)
	third & other	1.4% (15)	1.1% (11)	1.1 (11)	1.5% (15)
	(missing)	9.5% (100)	7.6% (77)	7.2% (74)	6.6% (66)
Race	white or Caucasian	62.1% (654)	62.6% (630)	65.8% (673)	62.2% (621)
	Black or African American	11.5% (121)	11.2% (113)	11.0% (112)	12.3% (123)
	American Indian or Alaska Native	0.5% (5)	0.8% (8)	0.9% (9)	0.8% (8)
	Asian or Asian American	4.5% (51)	5.9% (59)	5.6% (57)	6.4% (64)
	Native Hawaiian or Pacific Islander	0.4% (4)	0.8% (8)	0.4% (4)	0.8% (8)
	Latin or Hispanic	8.7% (92)	8.5% (86)	7.9% (81)	7.1% (7)
	Other	1.4% (15)	2.0% (20)	0.9% (9)	1.9% (19)
	Prefer not to say	1.3% (14)	0.6% (6)	0.7% (7)	1.7% (17)
	(missing)	9.2% (97)	7.7% (77)	6.9% (71)	6.7% (67)

Education				
Less than HS	9.2% (97)	7.4% (74)	9.9% (101)	8.2% (82)
HS, GED, vocational	26.9% (283)	18.9% (190)	21.5% (220)	19.9% (199)
Some college, no degree	22.5% (237)	27.5% (277)	24.9% (255)	23.6% (235)
Aassociate degree	11.5% (121)	13.6% (137)	13.8% (141)	11.3% (113)
College degree	17.57% (185)	23.1% (233)	19.8% (203)	27.2% (271)
Graduate degree	11.5% (121)	8.9% (90)	9.5% (97)	9.5% (95)
Other	0.9% (9)	0.6% (6)	0.6% (6)	0.3% (3)

Figure 3 Three screenshots of the one-minute video vignette

First Question

The first question was worded as followed: "Please indicate your level of agreement with the chief's handling of the body-worn camera footage." Respondents' choices were "strongly agree," "agree," "somewhat agree," "somewhat disagree," "disagree," or "strongly disagree."

Overall, across all experimental conditions, the median answers were the same for Americans at large and the residents of the three metro areas: the respondent at the 50th percentile agreed with the chief's handling. This distribution is somewhat surprising, in that 60 percent of the sample was not shown a video, yet they still agreed with the chief's handling. Figure 4 shows the levels of agreement with the chief's handling of the BWC video footage for all four samples, by experimental condition.

The patterns of agreement between the 40 percent of respondents who saw the BWC footage and the 60 percent of the respondents who did not see the footage was the same across all four samples. The difference in agreement between the respondents who saw the footage and the ones who did not was, on average, more than half a point from the six-point Likert scale, approaching half the standard deviation for all participants. For US residents at large, being assigned to one of the three control conditions lowered the level of agreement by .53 (t = −6.03). For residents of Seattle, the difference was −.61 (t = −7.0); in Los Angeles, it was −.65 (t = −7.82); and in Charlotte, it was −.59 (t = −6.59).

US residents at large tended to agree with the police chief's handling of BWC footage less than those who saw the footage, if the reason was that an investigation was pending. However, that difference is not large enough to be statistically significant. That pattern does not hold for Seattle, Los Angeles, and Charlotte, where respondents provided with that explanation tended to agree less than the treatment group by half a point of the six-item Likert scale. The results can be seen in Figure 5.

In these three cities, the differences were all statistically significant. In the United States at large, not releasing BWC footage after a fatal incident for mental health issues was seen as a less motivated exception than a pending internal investigation. That was not true in the three cities we surveyed. For Seattle and Charlotte, respondents agreed with the chief's handling of the BWC footage less than their peers who saw the footage. Not being able to see BWC footage because the officer did not activate their BWC lowered the agreement of respondents by 1.5 points or more, compared with participants who saw the BWC footage. That is the largest effect we collect from the other explanations. The nature of that reason is that BWC footage will never be seen, versus viewing merely being postponed as for a pending internal investigation. That is why respondents who otherwise

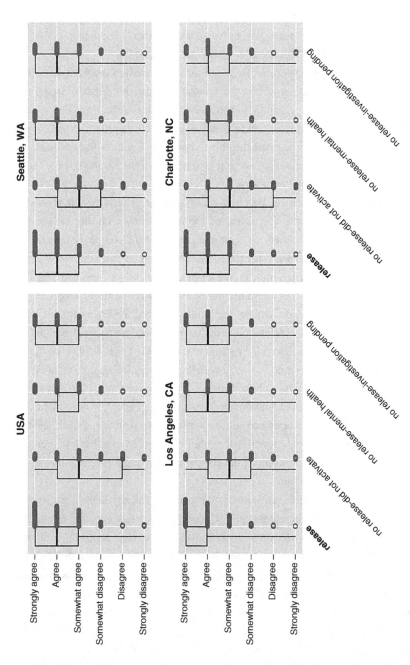

Figure 4 Distribution of agreements of respondents of the police chief's handling of the BWC footage, by sample and by experimental condition,

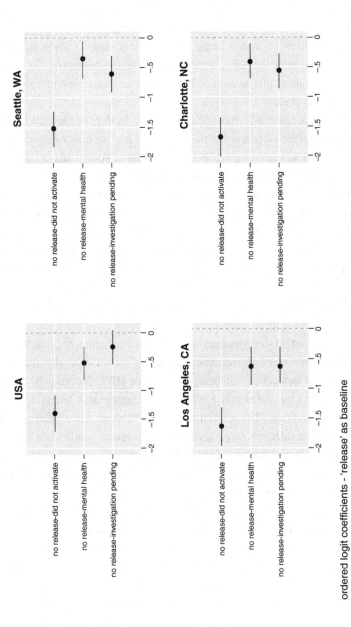

Figure 5 Effect of experimental condition on respondents' agreement with the chief's handling of BWC for those who did not see it, compared to those who did, by samples, unweighted

agreed or somewhat agreed when they saw the footage, somewhat agreed or somewhat disagreed when provided with that reason.

Second Question

The second of three prompts following the video vignette was the following: "On a scale from 0–10 with 0 being not transparent and 10 being extremely transparent, please rate the police department's level of transparency in disclosing information about this incident." The possible answers were offered in the form of a sliding scale.

When the three reasons for not seeing the BWC footage of the fatal incident are grouped together, 60 percent of those sampled find the police department to be significantly less transparent. For the 40 percent of Americans at large who could see the BWC footage, their mean assessment of transparency was at 7.7 from the 0–10 scale. The 60 percent of Americans at large who could not see the BWC footage for one the three reasons rated the police department's transparency at 5.8. The difference between the control groups and the treatment group was −1.92 points (t = −11.18). This pattern holds for respondents in the three cities. The difference between the respondents who saw the BWC footage of the fatal encounter and those who did not is −1.57 points in Seattle (t = −9.34), −2.16 points in Los Angeles (t = −13.23), and −1.76 points in Charlotte (t = −10.23).

The distribution of transparency assessments in Figure 6 illustrates the differences in perceived transparency according to reasons why the BWC footage was not available. Not being able to see BWC because the camera was not activated translates into a much lower transparency assessment than does seeing the footage. The general patterns of transparency assessments are the same for US residents at large, and for the residents of Seattle, Los Angeles, and Charlotte. US residents at large and residents of Charlotte register two quartiles, 50 percent of the population, who assess the police department as more opaque than transparent when the BWC was not activated.

From Figure 7, we can see that Angelinos are the ones more sensitive to not being able to see the BWC footage, as they find their police chief less transparent by two increments, instead of one and a half, as in Seattle and Charlotte. Their transparency rating falls the most of all four samples. Residents of Seattle are the ones whose assessments decrease the least, and the 20 percent of the sample in the "no release because the BWC did not activate" still rate their police department two full points lower than the treatment group who saw the footage. In the United States at large and in Charlotte and Los Angeles, the drop of 2.5 points is approximately the same as one standard deviation. Americans at large are also the ones less convinced by a mental health exception.

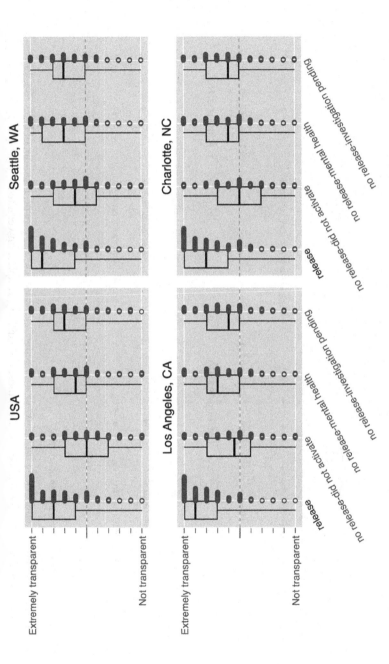

Figure 6 Distribution of transparency assessment of the police department's handling of BWC for those who did not see it, compared to those who did, by samples, unweighted

Police department's level of transparency in disclosing the BWC footage

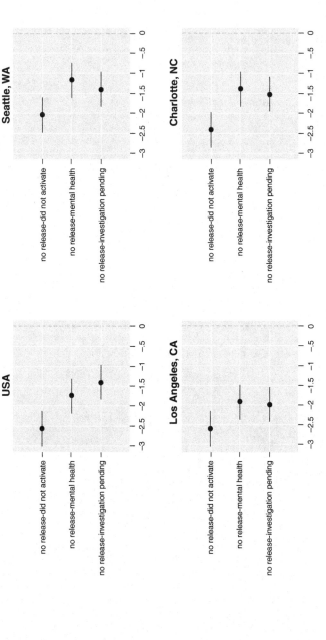

OLS coefficients - 'release' as baseline

Figure 7 Effect of experimental condition on transparency assessment of the police department' handling of BWC for those who did not see it, compared to those who did, by samples, unweighted

Third Question

The last of three questions recalls the question asked of police chiefs in Section 2. Respondents were asked: "Which of the following statements best captures your opinion of how a police department should release body-worn camera footage? (choose only one)." In answering this question, they could select from four options.

The distribution presented in Table 7 shows some overall (Design-based F = 3.06; Pr = .0011) differences. There is a slight preference in Seattle for a narrated version of the footage, and a slight preference in Charlotte for seeing the raw footage immediately, as revealed by multinominal regressions (not shown). However, these slight differences were not present with the unweighted data. One BWC footage release policy is clearly less popular than the others: where police departments would not release the footage, over all samples and for three of the four experimental conditions, less than 10 percent of respondents' preferences were for the police department not to the release the footage. For the respondents who were told they could not see the BWC footage because of a mental health issue, almost 20 percent expressed, "The police department should not release the footage" as their policy preference. Moreover, only 20 percent of the same respondents in this experimental condition, selected the option of seeing the raw footage immediately, opposed to 30 percent or more, as was the case for the other experimental conditions. That priming effect is large. These differences are the only statistically significant ones (respectively 286.5 percent, z = 8.69, and −74.1 percent; z = −8.69).

A stunning result is how stable the preferences are across samples. Across three widely different police department models presented in the literature, the respondents expressed roughly the same preferences. Interestingly, only 22.6 percent of Angelinos (20.7 percent in the unweighted data) selected "The police department should release a narrated version of the footage of the encounter so the public understands police procedures." As such, this practice from the LAPD might stem from police management's preferences and capacity versus citizens' preferences.

Trust as an Antecedent

Two measures of trust were used to assess residents' confidence in their police department. Respondents were asked about their confidence in policing in their own community. They were asked to express themselves on the two dimensions of the Perceptions of Police Scale (POPS) (Nadal and Davidoff 2015): the nine items for General Attitudes toward Police dimension and the three items for the

Table 7 Distribution of BWC footage release preferences, by weighted sample

	US	Seattle, WA	Los Angeles, CA	Charlotte, NC
The police department should not release the footage	9.8% (103)	10.7% (103)	7.0% (95)	8.0% (90)
The police department should release the raw footage of the encounter once an internal investigation is over	40.6% (427)	37.7% (357)	37.6% (375)	36.3% (379)
The police department should release a narrated version of the footage of the encounter so the public understands police procedures	17.3% (182)	23.6% (228)	22.6% (212)	20.0% (223)
The police department should immediately release the raw footage of the encounter	25.7% (271)	25.3% (265)	27.4% (282)	33.7% (259)
(missing)	6.6% (70)	2.8% (54)	5.3% (59)	2.2% (47)

Perceptions of Bias dimension. A higher score on the General Attitudes toward Police dimension denotes a more positive attitude; a higher score on Perceptions of Bias denotes a perception of an unbiased police department. Additionally, four items from a 2016 Pew Research Center study titled "The Racial Confidence Gap in Police Performance" were used individually, as they measure dimensions of accountability following misconduct, use of force, treating racial and ethnic groups equally, and protecting people from crime. Table 8 presents the mean and median scores for each of the four samples, by white and minority status.

What is striking from the six trust scores in Table 8 is how little variation there is from sample to sample. White Americans at large – or white residents from Seattle, Los Angeles, or Charlotte – have the same levels of trust in their police departments. The same is true for people of color among the four samples. Unsurprisingly, respondents of color tend to trust their police departments slightly less than whites do. The difference between the median white respondent and the respondent of color at the 50th percentile varies for the belief that misbehaving officers are held accountable and for using the right amount of force. Whites rate their departments as "good" on these two dimensions. People of color rate them as "average." The more important substantive difference between whites and people of color surrounds the Beliefs about Police Bias: the typical white respondent "somewhat agrees" that their department is free of bias; the typical person of color responded "somewhat disagrees."

As for policy preferences, Figure 8 presents the preferred video footage policy, the same information as in Table 8, but for white and minority respondents separately, by sample.

In all four samples, respondents of color prefer to see the BWC footage right away, compared with white respondents; they are also relatively less likely to want to wait until after an internal investigation to see BWC footage. These differences of preferences between whites and people of color are important ones. Again, there is a national consensus. Local differences are negligible.

In Tables 9 and 10, we attempt to examine whether levels of trust can help predict one's policy preferences toward accessing BWC footage. Tables 9 and 10 recall a similar analysis with police chiefs in Section 2. Table 10 presents the coefficients of a multinomial regression of citizens' general attitudes toward the police and perceptions of bias, the two POPS trust measures. Table 10 does the same with the four measures borrowed from PEW.

The relative probability of not wanting the footage released rather than accessing the raw footage immediately is 112.9 percent lower for minority residents who perceive their department as biased compared with minority residents who see their police department as unbiased. That probability is also lower for white residents who view their police department as biased, at

Table 8 Distribution of POPS "General Attitudes toward Police dimension," "General Attitudes toward Police," and Pew's "The Racial Confidence Gap in Police Performance," by unweighted sample and minority status.

		United States		Seattle, WA		Los Angeles, CA		Charlotte, NC	
		white	**POC**	**white**	**POC**	**white**	**POC**	**white**	**POC**
POPS (1 = strongly disagree, 6 = strongly agree)	Attitudes toward law enforcement Cronbach alpha=.96	4.57 ≈ agree	4.27 ≈ some-what agree	4.56 ≈ agree	4.26 ≈ some-what agree	4.57 ≈ agree	4.28 ≈ some-what agree	4.56 ≈ agree	4.24 ≈ some-what agree
	Beliefs about police bias (3 items) Cronbach alpha=.93	3.59 ≈ some-what agree	3.34 ≈some-what disagree	3.62 ≈ some-what agree	3.34 ≈ some-what disagree	3.61 ≈ some-what agree	3.38 ≈ some-what disagree	3.60 ≈ some-what agree	3.34 ≈ some-what disagree
PEW (1 = terrible, 5 = excellent) Cronbach alpha=.91	Holding officers accountable when misconduct occurs	3.48 good	3.28 average	3.51 good	3.27 average	3.50 good	3.28 average	3.49 good	3.25 average

Using the right amount of force for each situation	3.48 good	3.34 average	3.58 good	3.33 average	3.58 good	3.34 average	3.56 good	3.30 average
Treating racial and ethnic groups equally	3.41 average	3.18 average'	3.42 average	3.17 average	3.43 average	3.19 average	3.40 average	3.16 average
Protecting people from crime	3.73 good	3.56 good	3.73 good	3.55 good	3.74 good	3.57 good	3.73 good	3.52 good

Mean score (median in text). POC = person of color.

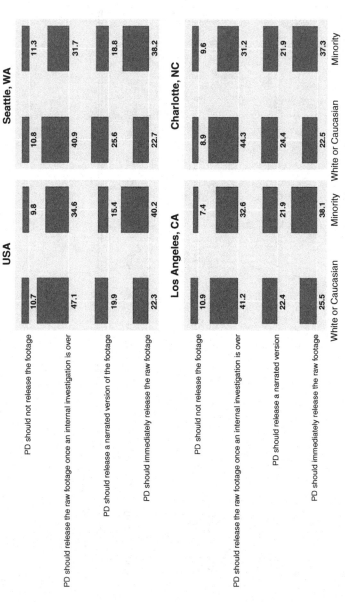

Figure 8 Distribution BWC footage release preferences, by sample and minority status, in percentage, unweighted

Table 9 Results of multinomial regression of citizens' general attitudes toward the police and perceptions of bias, by minority status, releasing raw footage immediately as the base outcome, with weighted data

Preference for BWC footage policy	Variables	Participants who are POC percentage odds ratio (std. err)	Participants who are white percentage odds ratio (std. err)
PD should not release the footage	General Attitudes	n.s.	n.s.
vs.	toward Police	(n.s.)	(n.s.)
PD should immediately release the raw footage of the	Perceptions of Bias	112.9%***	59.7%**
encounter		(0.21)	(0.15)
PD should release the raw footage of the encounter after	General Attitudes	n.s.	60.3%***
internal investigation	toward Police	(n.s.)	(0.11)
vs.	Perceptions of Bias	n.s.	n.s.
PD should immediately release the raw footage of the		(n.s.)	(n.s.)
encounter			
PD should release a narrated version of the footage of the	General Attitudes	85.6%**	74.8%***
encounter to the public	toward Police	(0.23)	(0.12)
vs.	Perceptions of Bias	n.s.	n.s.
PD should immediately release the raw footage of the		(n.s.)	(n.s.)
encounter			
Adjusted count R^2		n = 1105	n = 2487
		0.04	0.04

* $p < 0.05$; ** $p < 0.01$; *** $p < 0.001$

Table 10 Results of multinomial regression of citizens' four assessments of "The Racial Confidence Gap in Police Performance," by minority status, releasing raw footage immediately as the base outcome

Preference for BWC footage policy	Variables	Participants who are POC — Percentage odds ratio (std. err)	Participants who are white — Percentage odds ratio (std. err)
PD should not release the footage	Holding officers accountable when misconduct occurs	n.s. (n.s.)	56.7%** (0.15)
vs.	Using the right amount of force for each situation	n.s. (n.s.)	n.s. (n.s.)
PD should immediately release the raw footage of the encounter	Treating racial and ethnic groups equally	n.s. (n.s.)	63.4%** (0.16)
	Protecting people from crime	n.s. (n.s.)	n.s. (n.s.)
PD should release the raw footage of the encounter after internal investigation	Holding officers accountable when misconduct occurs	n.s. (n.s.)	n.s. (n.s.)
vs.	Using the right amount of force for each situation	n.s. (n.s.)	28.8%** (0.10)
PD should immediately release the raw footage of the encounter	Treating racial and ethnic groups equally	n.s. (n.s.)	n.s. (n.s.)
	Protecting people from crime	n.s. (n.s.)	n.s. (n.s.)

PD should release a narrated version of the footage of the encounter to the public

vs.

PD should immediately release the raw footage of the encounter

Holding officers accountable when misconduct occurs	n.s. (n.s.)	n.s. (n.s.)
Using the right amount of force for each situation	n.s. (n.s.)	37.4%*** (0.12)
Treating racial and ethnic groups equally	n.s. (n.s.)	32.4%*** (0.11)
Protecting people from crime	n.s. (n.s.)	n.s. (n.s.)
	$n = 1,122$	$n = 2,557$
Adjusted count R^2	0.01	0.05

* $p < 0.05$; ** $p < 0.01$; *** $p < 0.001$

59.7 percent. The relative probability of wanting to access the raw footage after an internal investigation rather than accessing the raw footage immediately is not higher for residents of color who view their police department positively compared with residents of color who do not. That probability is even higher for white residents at 60.3 percent. The relative probability of preferring to access a narrated version of the footage rather than accessing the raw footage immediately is 70.5 percent higher for residents of color who view their police department positively than for residents of color who do not. That probability is even higher for white residents at 67.0 percent. Perception of biases in one's police department only helps to explain why some respondents are satisfied with not seeing BWC footage. It does not predict policy preferences for either white respondents or respondents of color.

White respondents who more strongly agree that officers are held accountable when misconduct occurs are 56.7 percent more likely to prefer that footage not be released rather than accessing the raw footage immediately, compared with white respondents who are less sure that officers are held accountable when misconduct occurs. White respondents who more strongly believe that the right amount of force is used are 28.8 percent and 37.4 percent more likely, respectively, to prefer that the footage be released after an internal investigation or that a narrated version be accessed, compared with accessing the raw footage immediately – this compared with white respondents who are less sure that the right amount of force is used. Respectively, white respondents who more strongly believe that ethnic and racial groups are treated equally are 63.4 percent and 32.4 percent more likely to prefer that the footage not be released or that a narrated version be accessed, compared with accessing the raw footage immediately, this in comparison with white respondents who are less sure that ethnic and racial groups are treated equally. The trust that their police department is protecting people from crime is not a factor that helps explain why white respondents prefer one policy to another. None of these four measures of trust matters for respondents of color.

Discussion

This section started with a discussion about the lack of understanding of local preferences for BWC policies. The introduction mentioned that many models exist throughout the United States. One police chief who filled out the survey presented in Section 2 took the time to write us an email after completing our survey:

> The fundamental principle within law enforcement is that our system relies on the consent of the governed. The people within a community must consent to being policed. It is not forced upon them and should never be. This results in

citizens having the ultimate say in how their law enforcement agency will serve them. Each community will get exactly the policing they request from their law enforcement services. This is NOT dictated by the government or the police department, but rather the people being served. So, good or bad, the community is going to get exactly the type of policing they request. The law enforcement officers serving a community are merely a reflection of the community itself. (A police chief from a Californian city of <50,000 residents)

His point of view is that policies reflect local preferences.

We surveyed 4,000 residents, 1,000 residents from the United States at large and 1,000 from each of three cities with widely different BWC footage-sharing policies. Our results are that with very few exceptions, respondents react to reasons why they cannot see BWC of a fatal encounter in the same way. They assess the transparency of their department in the same manner. They have the same levels of trust toward their department. And, more importantly, they have the same policy preferences about when to access BWC footage. In our four samples, local preferences reflect a national consensus rather than local sensibilities and particularities.

Residents tended to be supportive of the police chiefs' decisions. Obviously, that was especially true for the respondents assigned to the experimental condition where they could see the BWC footage of the fatal encounter right away. The respondents from all four samples assigned to the condition where they could not see the BWC footage because the camera was not activated showed an important drop in agreement with the police chief's handling of the BWC footage. The support was lower for the 60 percent of respondents who could not see the footage right away. For a third of the respondents told that the camera was not activated, the mean support was much lower. The answers could be very negative for a fraction of respondents around the 25th percentile. For the two-thirds of respondents who could not see the BWC footage, waiting for the end of the internal investigation or being told that an exception was being made for mental health issues, support was lower than for those who saw the raw footage right away. That being said, support here was higher than for the respondents who were told that the camera was not activated. The same pattern holds regarding the assessment of transparency. US residents at large are more forgiving than the respondents from Seattle, Los Angeles, and Charlotte in relation to having to wait to see BWC footage after an internal investigation. However, they are less moved by the mental health argument.

By a large margin, respondents of color tend to want the raw BWC footage immediately. White respondents tend to be more trusting of the police and willing to wait for an internal investigation before viewing BWC footage. Nevertheless, trust plays a role in predicting policy preferences. The POPS indices are better predictors of policy preferences than the four measures from Pew. White respondents and respondents of color who have higher trust in the police, either via their general attitudes or belief that their police departments are not biased against minorities, are more likely to be at ease with never seeing the footage, seeing a narrated version of it, or waiting for the end of an internal investigation. The same dynamics for higher trust, through the four PEW measures tuned toward excessive force and accountability, hold for white respondents. However, they do not for minority respondents.

Conclusion

In a recent article, Graham and colleagues (2019) stated that citizens now expect to see BWC of all lethal uses of force from police officers: "When a police-citizen encounter goes awry, African Americans – and undoubtedly Americans in general – want to see what happened with their own eyes. In the current postfactual era where truth is devalued by partisan politicians and the media, anything short of this visual standard lacks credibility" (p. 298). Our research examines what citizens in the United States at large and in three cities expect in terms of access to BWC footage. A surprising result is that the preferred BWC policy, by a large minority, is to wait until an internal investigation is over before seeing footage. This is true for US residents at large but also for respondents from the three cities. The results differ from the self-selected participants of the LAPD and NYPD consultations (Policing Project 2018a, 2018b), who expressed a preference for seeing raw footage as soon as possible. What we found is that trusting residents and white residents are comfortable with letting their police departments finish an internal investigation before being allowed to see BWC footage.

McElroy (2019) made a prediction about the footage release policy in Charlotte:

> The technology is only as strong as the policies and leaders who govern it. By removing decision making from the hands of law enforcement, the new law in North Carolina may create delays that will exacerbate the problems and perhaps detract from law enforcement's best intentions for BWCs: to build trust with the community. (McElroy 2019a)

To that effect, our results show that various measures of trust in the police in Charlotte are the same as in Los Angeles, Seattle, and the United States at large. One of the reasons suggested for BWCs not increasing trust in some communities is that citizens cannot access footage (Sellick 2019). Another possibility is that the use of BWC does not build trust with the community, as a recent study of forty residents of Washington, DC, found (Wright and Headley 2020 p. 7). Another suggestion – buttressed with the example of Axon hiring the Pittsburgh police commander to lobby Pennsylvania's State Legislature to make BWC footage inaccessible to the public – is that BWCs are not meant to build community trust but to enhance public relations (Stroud 2019, p. 207). However, our analyses could not parse out that last element.

The CPA model is used to predict the behavior of the actor being held to account – not the forum holding the actor accountable. That said, the model offers propositions that are contingent on the actor better understanding the forum's preferences. Further, based on our findings from Section 2, we know that trust shifts a police chief's willingness to disclose footage. Trust is a relational concept. Therefore, understanding the forum's trust levels and policy preferences will help explain the actor's behavior. While a theoretical model like the CPA can predict behavior regardless of inputting a forum's preferences, its practical relevance is limited without this knowledge. Ultimately, these empirical findings can point us toward a policy solution.

5 *356 Different* Stories about BWC?

Introduction

In their 2020 book aimed at synthesizing the flow of BWC research, White and Malm (2020) mention the following: "While there will not be eighteen thousand different BWC stories [representing the 18,000 police departments,] there will certainly be more than one, and in fact, there may be many" (p. 16). In this section, we will present the stories gathered from many hundreds of police chiefs, some of whose departments have BWCs. The narratives let police chiefs explain how their relationships within their departments and with their stakeholders, as well as accountability holders, were changed or would be changed by BWCs.

In a recent research study combing through the LEMAS-BWCS – a survey of 15,328 general-purpose law enforcement agencies done in 2016 and published by the Bureau of Justice Statistics in 2018, J. Smith (2019, p. 380) notes that future research should include in-depth qualitative case studies of police departments that have chosen not to adopt BWCs. Therefore, this study includes both those departments that have adopted BWCs and those that have not.

Accountability can be defined as a social relationship in which one actor feels an obligation to explain and to justify their conduct to some significant other (Bovens , 2005, p. 184). This is dependent on two factors. First, there is an agreed-upon set of criteria, and second, when one strays from those criteria, they feel obliged to explain their conduct. In the case of policing, as with many public services, there are many actors to whom one might feel an obligation to justify their behavior and there are many rules and norms to which one must abide.

In this section, we aim at understanding the effect of BWCs on the relationships that form the basis of accountability. To whom do chiefs feel accountable? How do they see BWCs affecting these accountability relationships? In Sections 2 and 3, we examined polices and behavior related to the release of video footage. We did this from the perspective of both citizens and police chiefs. In this section, we dig deeper into how BWCs help shape those perspectives.

Methodology and Analyses

Our goal in this survey was to get police chiefs, or other heads of agencies, to speak openly about the effects of BWCs on their relationships within their organizations and their communities. The design was inspired by the work of Halley and colleagues (2018), who analyzed hundreds of qualitative narratives from physicians who are mothers. Therefore, our survey was framed with the following statement:

> Both smartphone and body-worn cameras increasingly film police officers. The footage provides civilians with selected views of law enforcement in the United States. Video footage is also shared through social media and mainstream media increasing circulation and viewership. We want to hear your story.

We then posed the questions, which were adjusted for departments with cameras and departments without cameras. Additionally, we randomly assigned chiefs into one of two groups. The randomization was done to neutralize the order effect of elements in the question. The first group received a question in which we asked about relationships with fellow officers first and citizens second, and the second group received a question with the opposite order. The language of the question in the first group is as follows:

> Please share the impacts body-worn cameras have had on the behavior in your department. How have they affected your supervisory relationship with your officers? How have they impacted your relationship with the citizens you serve? Please feel free to discuss any or all of these topics. You may also share any other impacts you think are relevant.

The language of the question in the second group was as follows:

> Please share the impacts body-worn cameras have had on the behavior in your department. How have they affected your relationship with the citizens you serve? How have they affected your supervisory relationship with your officers? Please feel free to discuss any or all of these topics. You may also share any other impacts you think are relevant.

The survey was sent to 5,723 police chiefs. This sample was drawn from the same database as in Section 2 but represents the second half of the list.

Therefore, these chiefs were different from those contacted in Section 2. While 509 respondents began the survey, 356 completed it. Hence the n for this study is 356 respondents with a response rate of 6.2 percent. We were expecting a lower response rate than that reported in Section 2 since providing a narrative is more demanding than answering multiple-choice questions in a typical survey. Our goal was to obtain as many narratives as possible; it was not to maximize the response rate. We have responses from every state except Alaska and Hawaii. The mean population served by the police or sheriff's department was slightly more than 36,000 people, whereas the median was 9,000 people. The minimum population in a jurisdiction was five people and the maximum was nearly 2 million. The chiefs represented departments that had average of 41 officers with a median of 18. The largest agency a chief represented had more than 2,500 officers and the smallest agency had one officer. The responses were then coded by three coders in Dedoose, software for qualitative analysis. Codes were compared. Any discrepancies were discussed and adjusted.

The coding took place in three stages. The first stage of coding was based on the level of analysis in the chief's response. We asked: how is the chief viewing these relationships? Are their responses framed by societal relationships, community relationships, institutional relationships, or individual relationships? The initial round of coding demonstrated a clear focus on institutions. This is not surprising based on the questions and the way they were posed, but it provides a basic understanding of police chiefs' mind-sets. Chiefs generally referenced institutional factors in response to the posed questions. In total, 317 cases received codes; 277 of those cases had an institutional code present. Chiefs discussed the cost of cameras, training opportunities, how cameras are used to address complaints from residents, legal responses, administrative burdens, and opportunities. The next most prevalent category that chiefs discussed was the community. A total of 207 cases coded had a "community" code present. In general, these were comments related to how BWCs have affected these relationships and the perspectives related to cameras. Chiefs discussed cameras protecting officers from inaccurate citizen complaints and citizens appreciating the transparency. A total of 130 of the cases had the prevalence of codes at the individual level. In these cases, chiefs referenced officers' behavior. Rather than discussing the community or citizens in general, they were focusing on how individuals behaved. Common responses in this category included behavior of officers with the public, retraining specific officers, and dealing with complaints against officers. The last category in assessing the unit of analysis was societal. This was coded as a level higher than community. There were 97 cases that had the prevalence of a "societal" code. A societal code was given when a chief referenced something larger than their organization or community responses alone. A response might have included a reference to broader societal trends surrounding social media or the broader idea of public accountability.

The second round of coding utilized the existing framework employed by Mark Bovens (2007). We looked at bureaucratic, legal, political, administrative, and professional accountability categories. The most prevalent code in round two was bureaucratic. It occurred in 239 cases. These cases referenced bureaucratic processes, supervisory activities, and citizen complaints. The most prevalent cases were related to citizen complaints and efficiency in dismissing these cases. The code of professional was the second most prevalent code with 120 occurrences. These responses referenced three main ideas. First, officers behave in a professional manner, and videos do not have any effect. Second, BWCs ensure that the "bad apples" behave in a professional manner. Third, BWCs ensure that both officers and citizens have polite and professional encounters. There were 88 cases coded with the occurrence of a legal code. A response coded in this manner dealt specifically with the legal apparatus. There might have been reference to a prosecutor or to a judge. Chiefs would also reference the video footage with the term "evidence." The code "political" was present in 68 cases. These narratives focused on the demand for information. While some mentioned the increased administrative burden this caused, many others mentioned that it provided an opportunity to be transparent. The last category of "administrative" received few codes. In total, 25 cases had the presence of an administrative code. These relatively few cases referred to administrative processes, internal affairs, and accreditation.

In round three, we parsed the narrative one step further to understand the people referenced in the accountability relationship. In this round, we looked for words like "supervisor," "citizens," "prosecutor" (or court official), "auditors," and "peers." The most frequently identified codes were those of peers (or fellow officers), citizens, and supervisors. Each of these categories had prevalence of about 150–165 identified cases. The other categories all received fewer than 30 codes.

We learned a great deal about how police chiefs view the use of BWCs. While ideas about transparency and accountability run through the chiefs' responses, BWCs are viewed primarily as a tool to help them do their jobs better. Moreover, an emergent theme in the responses speaks to a sense of vindication. Hence, when we are thinking about to whom and for what police officers are accountable, it becomes clear that there is an internal sense of justice to which police chiefs subscribe. This sense does not preclude transparency to the broader community. In many cases, chiefs suggest that it increases transparency

However, accountability is viewed less in relation to what citizens want and more to what the profession demands. The standard story is captured well by a police chief from a community of 6,200 residents:

> We all understand that body cameras can be a deterrent for bad behavior. My officers love wearing the cameras and it is the first thing that they grab when they come to work. If, like in my department, you have officers that are out being professional and doing their jobs, they value it as a true form of transparency into what actually took place. The citizens that are law abiding enjoy the transparency provided by their police department. (Case 410, Seven Officers, with BWC)

The behavior the chief describes is one part of a multidimensional relationship. It begins with a professional officer and ends with a law-abiding citizen. If every interaction between police and citizens began and ended this way, the calls for BWCs would likely not have occurred. Others note that while the goal is to have a professional interaction, sometimes that does not happen. As another chief notes, "we are human" (Case 207, 20 Officers, with BWC). Therefore, a more nuanced perspective offered by a chief of a municipality of 22,000 residents suggests the BWC plays a role in this behavior:

> I believe that BWCs have been well received by our officers. More often than not it demonstrates that officers are out in the field doing the job they are expected to do and in a professional manner. Typically if there is an issue it relates to the officer being rude or not conducting themselves in a professional manner. Furthermore, it holds both the officer and the contact accountable for their respective behavior. (Case 276, with BWC)

This more nuanced response suggests that the camera can be used as a tool to hold officers and residents accountable for their behavior. But for what are they being held accountable to – professionalism? One chief, recounting a story from one of his officers, suggests that civility and professionalism might be the incentivized behavior:

> Officers say it simplifies investigations and gives both the citizens and officers incentive to be civil. A direct quote from one of my officers recently when I received a complaint is "Please take a look at the body camera video. The contact was perfectly professional. By the way, I love these cameras. They are great to protect us against false complaints." (Case 373, 23 Officers, with BWC)

What emerges in the chiefs' comments are the dynamics of interactions between residents and police – not the details of these interactions, but the idea that there may be an us-against-them mentality. This is confirmed throughout the responses, and while not always explicit, the data points to the prominence of this belief. A police chief from a small community of 2,500 further articulates these dynamics:

> We hire independent-thinking officers who operate under a broad umbrella of permissible actions, as long as what they are doing is legal, moral, and ethical. For instance, if someone is busy lobbing F-bombs and verbally accosting them, they are expected to remain professional but have the discretion to talk back in kind. That behavior won't change with body cameras, except to showcase public behaviors vs police professionalism. (Case 413, without BWC)

This quote is distinct from the other narratives we received while highlighting one of the major themes. Commonly, it highlights an adversarial relationship. What is not common in the narratives offered by other police chiefs is the idea that "behavior won't change." Rather, there is a general theme that behavior will change both for officers and for citizens. As one chief notes:

> The effect on the officer's behavior has been positive as they know they are going to be held accountable for their actions more so than at any other time in their careers. I think with this mindset, officers are providing better service to our populace. (Case 446, 65 Officers, with BWC)

Another chief writes:

> Accountability has been the largest impact that I have seen. The department (supervisors) are holding their officers more accountable through video reviews. The officers are aware, most of the time, that at least one camera is rolling on them and this seems to change behavior. (Case 220, 20 Officers, with BWC)

This behavior change is consistent with the CPA model, in that civilians and officers are shaping and reshaping their interactions. Officers are learning what this forum – community residents – expects and adjusting their behaviors accordingly. Chiefs are also taking an active role in modifying behavior. Training of officers is a common theme that chiefs note:

> Supervisory wise all Patrol Lieutenants are responsible for command of patrol officers must randomly video each officer in their command at least once a month. They are looking for training issues and any other issues that may arise. All use of force videos are reviewed by supervisors, department use of force instructors and the Office of Responsibility to ensure compliance with policy and law. (Case 168, 69 Officers, with BWC)

A different chief noted the following:

> The BWC increases professionalism in policing. Officers are aware of their actions and the language they used. They are able to learn from reviewing

their performance in handling conflict or difficult situations. The BWC coverage provides supervisors with an independent perspective or view of situations, and it augments their ability to teach and coach officers, along with supporting their investigations of complaints or misconduct. (Case 371, Population more than 1.5 million, with BWC)

This enhanced role that supervisors are playing has changed internal relationships between officers and supervisors. Supervisors are able to offer more guidance and training to help lower-rank officers. However, aspects of this relationship forming may reinforce the us-against-them narrative. One chief said, "During the initial implementation of the program, our focus was to obtain buy-in from the officers. We gained acceptance and support from most of the officers by showing them how body-worn cameras validate good officer behavior" (Case 27, 44 Officers, with BWC). This validation is not only for an external audience. Speaking of the internal dynamic, a chief says, "The supervisory relationship with officers seemed to improve after we launched the program. I feel in part that this happened, because it allowed officers to be cleared in the vast majority of complaints due to having videos to back up their side of the incident in question" (Case 44, 10 Officers, with BWC).

Many of the responses hinge on a similar logic and point to what seems to be the most common use of BWCs – to process citizen complaints. In more than 130 cases, the respondents mention citizen complaints, and a typical response sounds similar to how a chief from a municipality of more than 25,000 people puts it: "First and foremost, the cameras have aided in handling complaints on officers' behavior and actions during interaction with both citizens and persons being arrested" (Case 446, Texas, with BWC). The responses then range in extremes. Some offer an absolute perspective, such as a chief from a municipality with 7,000 residents. He states, "Every Officer complaint has been ruled unsupported after reviewing the video footage" (Case 209, high levels of citizen trust). A chief of a community of 3,000 residents shared similar sentiment:

> Our Body Worn Cameras have been a great help in providing our admin staff with the truth of what's happening with our officer when they make contact with citizens. Our officers had a bad reputation; the body cameras have vindicated our officers' actions nearly 100 percent of the time. (Case 351, Southern United States, with BWC)

Some chiefs take a more cooperative approach to reviewing BWC footage in relation to citizen complaints. For example, one chief notes:

> The biggest thing that I have noticed the body-worn cameras help with is complaints and training. When we receive a complaint, we can easily review footage and close the complaint out more quickly and more accurately.

Supervisors love them for reviewing Use of Force incidents or any complaints. They have been very beneficial in clearing up incidents where a citizen may have questions. (Case 190, high levels of trust)

This was a frequent theme in responses. Another chief explained both the feelings of the officers and how supervisors might handle a complaint:

At first there were a few officers who were concerned. They felt that it was going to have supervisors second-guessing their work. However, after a while everyone began to appreciate the value of them. Citizen complaints were lessened. Citizens would call about an officer, a supervisor would say that it was all on video, and the subject would quite often withdraw their complaint, or change it from formal to informal. It has been a boon on the investigative front. Officers are able to review video to make sure their reports are as accurate as possible. The District Attorney's office likes it and cases with recordings seem to be less likely to go to court. (Case 375, high levels of trust)

There remains a perception, however, that citizens often withdraw complaints upon being confronted with BWC footage. As one chief puts it, "Also the accountability of our citizens, many times complaints seem to evaporate once the complainant knows we have footage of an encounter" (Case 220, 20 Officers, Southeastern United States). Ultimately, with the data that we have, it is impossible to know what the interaction between a complainant and an officer looks like. It seems, at the least, that complainants are confronted with videos of the incident and may decide to recant their stories. The description of these interactions is certainly a limit of this study. Was pressure applied during this interaction or did a resident simply have a change of heart? Did the video reveal behavior that one might not want aired publicly? According to our results, chiefs think that watching the footage provides a vantage point that is challenging to see while in the midst of engaging with an officer. As one chief puts it, "Perception is such a big part of our belief of what happened during an incident. Many people's perception is based off of emotion they were experiencing at the time. When they have either watched the video or had us explain what we saw it seems to calm them down" (Case 68, 10 Officers, Western United States). Another chief takes this slightly further:

When citizens do complain about an officer and we mention that we will review the video oftentimes they will re-evaluate their position. There have been times where I have sent the videos to the complainant and asked them to review it themselves and if they still feel strongly about what took place to let me know. When they have an opportunity to review the incident objectively after the fact they often see it in a different light. I believe that we have a strong relationship with the citizens that we serve because we have been transparent. More importantly when we are wrong, we will acknowledge it and address the matter. (Case 276, 37 Officers)

The insight gained from this data illustrates that a citizen complaint is an entry point to better understanding this relationship. It provides an opportunity for departments to have conversations with citizens about a situation and the facts surrounding the contact with the police. Chiefs believe this process builds trust. "BWCs are a tool and a program," one chief explains, "that support police department in building trust with the community, particularly in the review of critical incidents such as officer-involved shootings" (Case 371).

But these are complicated issues that cannot simply be resolved by video footage. Another chief references the physiological and mental components involved in a use of force incident:

BWCs are a great tool, but I believe the media and citizens rely on them to tell an entire story, when in reality it's just a small part of what is going on. If they were put in situations that had a similar mental and physiological impact and then record for them to watch at a later time, I believe they would understand much better. (Case 68, Western United States)

The chief is identifying an empathetic component to the BWC – putting oneself in another's shoes and gaining a better understanding of what is happening. But there is a risk to doing this. Police and residents often do not see a situation in the same manner. And, as many chiefs explain, the body-worn camera may deepen this divide:

BWCs were meant to help police departments build trust in the communities they serve. My experience has been that BWCs have done much more to damage trust than to build trust. We enjoy a good, trusting relationship with our citizens, but every time a new video surfaces depicting an officer taking action in the field, we come under scrutiny from news media and members of our community. Even when the officer's actions are justified and well within our policies for Response to Resistance (Use of Force), the news media and certain social groups find something to be upset about. This has impacted the way officers conduct themselves in the field. I am told they are afraid of becoming the next headline and so they feel reluctant and hesitant to use the force necessary to perform their job duties and keep our community safe. As a city, we are taking a more aggressive posture. When we have an incident involving force that we believe could be the next news story, we create our own video explaining in detail what happened and why the officer(s) took the actions they did. So far, we have found this to be effective in helping to ensure the truth is the first story our community hears; not some news media reporter's version of the truth. (Case 219 low level of citizen trust, population greater than 200,000)

The stance this chief is taking is that BWCs reduce trust. That leads to the question of whether authentic trust was present prior to BWCs.

More telling responses came from police chiefs who said very little has changed with the introduction of BWCs:

> Prior to the implementation of the BWCs we had spent many years molding officer behaviors to be more community oriented; thus when BWCs came into the mainstream we were already prepared and acting on positive and appropriate interactive behaviors. Same with relationships with citizens and supervisory staff. Nothing really changed. (Case 14, high levels of citizen trust)

Conclusion

Lum and colleagues (2019), after synthesizing the BWC literature and pointing out blind spots and gaps, surmise that BWCs will not increase accountability since supervision and mentorship are weak in some departments. The result, in some police departments, is that "the inability of BWCs to impact accountability structures may already be seen in findings that cameras are primarily used by the police (and prosecutors) to increase the accountability of citizens, not officers" (Lum et al. 2019, p. 109). This skeptical view of BWCs resonates with our findings. In many of the cases we examined, a police chief mentions the ability to hold citizens accountable for their behavior and the fact that BWC are used primarily to dismiss citizen complaints.

In theory, this represents "defense bolstering," which is articulated in both the CPA model and the contingency theory. The chief has no control of when a complaint will be filed. Hence, they do not know if or when they will be held accountable; a complaint is filed in the aftermath of an officer's perceived bad behavior. Rather than having a multidimensional response that is employed when a chief knows when they will be held accountable, they default to a defensive stance. However, evidence remains that chiefs have a desire to educate both law enforcement and civilians during this process.

In Section 1, we built upon the CPA model by adding a substantial component about trust. This proved to be a significant variable in both Sections 2 and 3. We described the scenario of trust development as that of two trading partners – haggling over a fair price. Once partners are comfortable with each other, haggling is no longer needed – trust is established. While haggling offers a straightforward example, the process is more iterative and complicated. Considering how social exchange works, people are constantly developing norms of behavior, and these norms emerge and solidify over multiple interactions (Thibaut and Kelley 1959). While we might assume that the norms between civilians and law enforcement are well established, this would be an inaccurate assumption. Mourtgos and Adams (2019) examined nearly thirty years of public perception of police use-of-force data. They conclude, "a sizeable portion of the American public disapproves of police use-of-force in situations in which such action would be legally and professionally reasonable" (p. 893). They go on to note, "Reducing the space between legal expectations on the one hand, and community expectations on the other, is an increasingly salient public policy priority" (p. 893).

What we have learned from police chiefs in this section is that norm creation is still taking place in many civilian-police interactions, and BWCs offer a tool to support this development. In filing a complaint, civilians are expressing their expectations for law enforcement behavior. The act of dismissing a complaint implies a chief does not agree with those expectations or that the legally established norms have not been broken. Both the chief and the complainant are establishing the terms of the relationship. If law enforcement takes the stance that officers will be vindicated 100 percent of the time, they are missing an opportunity to build trust. While one can understand why dismissing a complaint expediently might fit within a legal framework of accountability, this alone should not dictate the response. Rather, As Jos (2006) explains, "administrators are left to build consensus in cultural, political, and institutional settings that often work against shared commitments, settings over which they have little control" (p. 148). Footage from a BWC offers an opportunity to understand the other's perspective: "By attending to the contingent communicative acts through which public professionals and citizens interact in daily practice, we can come to an understanding of the actual consequences and value of their encounters" (Bartels 2013, p. 476). If law enforcement and civilians heed this advice, we can move from the haggling stage to the productive stage of a trusting relationship.

6 Conclusion: Calibrated Public Accountability: From a Model Toward a Theory

As Friedman (2017) reminds us, policing involves the use of force and surveillance, and that surveillance should be debated as much as the use of force (p. 311). This responsibility is especially important as policing "continues to move from a model that requires force to forestall and apprehend the bad guys, to one in which widespread surveillance is used to detect and prevent bad acts before they occur (Friedman 2017, p. 311). In this Element, we looked at just one narrow policy implementation of a technological solution: police body-worn cameras. We evaluated how this new form of accountability that has been taking place in policing – video footage of extreme and rare experiences, rather than aggregated and curated annual reports – can be explained by existing accountability frameworks.

What we found is a gap between the preferences of police chiefs and those of citizens in terms of accountability and transparency. That gap can be seen in table 11 by comparing the results of Sections 2 and 3. After an officer-involved shooting caught on camera, very few police chiefs favored showing the raw footage immediately. Something close to a majority of police chiefs favored releasing the BWC footage only after an internal investigation. Where the gulf widens is when we compare the preferences of police chiefs with the preferences of residents, separated by ethnic and racial minority status. Said differently, police chiefs' preferences were mostly in line with those of white residents in the United States and in the three cities we surveyed. However, residents of color, who expressed slightly less trust in their police departments than whites, were less willing to wait until the end of an internal investigation. A large minority of residents of color wanted to see the BWC footage right away, before the end of an internal investigation. Additionally, most of them preferred the raw footage to a stylized and/or narrated version of the footage. In this Element, we studied police chiefs, not police officers. As such, we did not delve into stories like the recent Washington, DC, Metropolitan Police Department officers' union that sued to delay a new law whereby BWC footage would be released within five days after an incident (DeMarco 2020).

As we reported in detail in Section 3, residents across three cities, with different accountability models, expressed similar expectations for BWC footage release and transparency. That held true for white residents and residents of color. There is a shared substantial consensus across the United States. The marked differences in release policies of BWC video footage across Seattle, Los Angeles, and Charlotte cannot be explained by the preferences expressed by our respondents from these three cities.

Trust mattered in explaining our results. For police chiefs, trust in the media and trust in community mattered to chiefs' preferred BWC policy choices, but only if they were in total control of the narrative – that is, if the BWC version was the only one in existence. If there was a version of the fatal shooting filmed by a smartphone, then the different kinds of trust harbored by chiefs did not matter. From the citizen's point of view, our more than 4,000 respondents were satisfied with waiting for the end of an internal investigation to see BWC footage if they had a positive attitude toward the police or believed that their police department was unbiased toward minorities. Still, from the citizen's point of view, one surprising element from Section 3 is how the police departments under study and all of the individual police departments from the representative sample of 1,000 Americans each registered the same scores in the trust measures from Pew

Table 11 Distribution of BWC footage release preferences in residents, and police chiefs recommendations, by sample and minority status, in percentage, with weighted data

The police department should…	United States		Seattle, WA		Los Angeles, CA		Charlotte, NC		Police chiefs
	white	POC	white	POC	white	POC	white	POC	
Not release the footage	9.9%	9.0%	10.3%	9.0%	9.0%	8.5%	9.4%	8.2%	12.5%
Release raw footage of the encounter after an internal investigation	43.2%	37.7%	42.5%	36.4%	42.9%	35.3%	41.7%	36.1%	48.7%
Release a narrated version of the footage of the encounter so the public understands police procedures	21.7%	20.9%	22.4%	22.1%	22.4%	21.5%	21.7%	21.6%	26.8%
Release raw footage of the encounter	25.1%	32.4%	24.4%	32.5%	22.5%	34.7%	27.2%	34.0%	12.2%

and the two indices from the POPS measures from white respondents and minority respondents. Something akin to the nationalization of politics, replacing local particularism – dubbed "McPolitics" by Mounk (2018) – might be at play. Citizens' trust in the police might have been nationalized and hence keeps tenuous links with what their own police departments are doing.

Our results show support for the two dimensions of the CPA model – anticipated accountability and the relationship between forum and actor. From the perspective of the police chiefs, our results demonstrate that when one can anticipate the timing of accountability, trust will play a factor in their response. Specifically, if police chiefs have the discretion to decide when to release footage, they will use trust to determine the immediacy of that release. The more trust the chiefs have in the residents of their community, the more likely they will be to release raw footage immediately.

Similarly, our findings support the conclusion that the relationship between the actor and the forum is important from the forum's perspective. When the forum has increased trust in the police, they are more likely to give the police time to conduct an internal investigation prior to releasing BWC footage. As trust decreases, the forum relinquishes that discretion and demands to see footage immediately.

"Body cameras . . . are one other means to try to keep policing within bounds as it regulates itself. No matter what the evidence proves in the long haul, the fundamental point is still the same: cameras are cameras; they are tools of assuring compliance, not governance" (Friedman 2017, p. 313). When levels of trust are heightened, assuring compliance is not a necessary mechanism.

The analyses from the hundreds of narratives we gathered from police chiefs added depth to our findings. These results revealed which audiences police chiefs see as their forums. They also demonstrate that much work remains to be done for citizens and law enforcement to see eye to eye on their interactions. If law enforcement views cameras as holding civilians accountable, and civilians view cameras as a manner to hold law enforcement accountable, the demands for BWC are creating a divide rather than building a bridge. If our goal is to bridge that divide, then cameras must be seen as a tool to hold officers and civilians accountable for a shared set of standards.

It has been suggested that once BWCs have been in place as a policing tool the technology cannot be rolled back without public pushback (Braunstein and Erickson 2019, p. 519), and that they will become a permanent part of policing in the United States and abroad (White and Malm 2020, p. 16). Others warn that the widespread use of BWCs will provide a treasure trove of data for those seeking to scrutinize every officer movement. The widespread existence of footage of police interactions will set the stage for the next wave of automation with ramifications that are not yet understood, via mission creep: "the process by which technology introduced for one purpose comes to be used for another" (Bowling and Iyer 2019, p. 155).

Students of Public Administration should heed Merton's (1940) warning of the "displacement of goals" in which "instrumental values" replace our "terminal values." While a lengthy aside, Merton's words are instructive:

> (1) An effective bureaucracy demands reliability of response and strict devotion to regulations. (2) Such devotion to the rules leads to their transformation into absolutes; they are no longer conceived as relative to a given set of purposes. (3) This interferes with ready adaptation under special conditions not clearly envisaged by those who drew up the general rules. (4) Thus, the very elements which conduce toward efficiency in general produce inefficiency in specific instances. Full realization of the inadequacy is seldom attained by members of the group who have not divorced themselves from the "'meanings" which the rules have for them. These rules in time become symbolic in cast, rather than strictly utilitarian. (p. 564)

The premise that Merton is articulating is one in which we lose sight of the broad goal of a public organization. If we lean too heavily on the use of BWC as "the solution," we will start to identify many problems that it may solve – independent of its original intended purpose. We fall into the familiar arguments of means and ends and have to remind ourselves of Dahl's (1947) insight "that science cannot demonstrate moral values, that science cannot construct a bridge across the great gap from 'is' to 'ought'" (p. 1). Further, we cannot divorce public administration from the "social, economic, and political environment" (p. 8). He writes, "A particular nation-state embodies the results of many historical episodes, traumas, failures, and successes which have in turn created peculiar habits, mores, institutionalized patterns of behavior" (p.8).

Simply because a tool has the *capability* of achieving a particular goal does not mean we *ought* to use that tool to achieve that goal. In Mary Franks's discerning law review article, she places surveillance in its historical context – specifically related to some of the most vulnerable populations in the United States: poor people of color (Franks 2017, p. 477).

BWCs, depending on how related policies and actual uses are implemented, can have a minimal impact on police accountability to the public, but they still increase government surveillance of the public, especially the urban poor (Chavis 2019, p. 452).

This mission creep has already started in places like St. Paul, Minnesota, where BriefCam, an algorithm that can generate searchable key terms from footage, can look for a "blue car" or "a man wearing a white shirt" at specific moments and places and is set up to enable facial recognition (Gottfriend

2020). In reaction to the spread of policing tools like BriefCam, the chief program officer for Minnesota's American Civil Liberties Union stated that the police department should "let community members provide input before implementing technologies like Briefcam" (Gottfriend 2020). Since it makes policing easier, it will change policing. The spread of Shotspotter, a technology that triangulates and alerts police departments of gun discharges, has already replaced tips from the community in many cities across the United States.

In an interview with Henderson County Sheriff Ed Brady, who heads a department where BWCs have been in use for eleven years, he stated that BWCs have only upsides, and no downsides (B. Smith 2019). He went on to pinpoint two reasons for seeing only upsides: "In many cases, if defense attorneys see video before trial, they settle. The second, if there is a citizen complaint, we can clear up most in five minutes. It's probably one of the best things we've done." With the right set of policies, BWCs can be just one more surveillance tool to make police departments more effective without making them more open, vulnerable, or accountable. It is not hyperbole to say that all police departments are under pressure to acquire and deploy BWCs, and in fact, if the Justice in Policing Act of 2020 passes, all federal police will be required to wear BWCs. Further, federal funding will be tied to local departments using BWCs. As Graham and colleagues (2019) note, "The impetus for all major police departments to implement BWCs thus is unlikely to subside in the foreseeable future" (p. 298). Again, and again, BWCs are seen as a way to boost legitimacy. However, Braga and Weisberg (2019) remind us that police legitimacy is a means of pursuing other goals, not the key goal: "The police are created to prevent crime, to respond to crimes, or to ensure order in the community, and so forth" (Braga and Weisberg 2019, p. 560). Legitimacy is a key element of policing a democratic society. Individuals who consider the police legitimate are more likely to cooperate and offer tips, as well as comply with directives and abide by the law (Worden and McLean 2017, pp. 6, 42). The same is true for other public agencies that do not garner support from parts of the population, be it the Environmental Protection Agency, the Centers for Disease Control, the Office of the State Comptroller, and so on. Procedural fairness and transparency might boost legitimacy in the eyes of many citizens. It might also assist agencies in achieving their objectives, but it is not the objective.

The results from our three empirical sections tested key parts of the CPA model, and considering our findings, we now move the Calibrated Public Accountability Model toward a Calibrated Public Accountability Theory. It reads as follows:

Given that a public manager expects they will be held accountable for a specific act, they will engage in a multidimensional response to a forum. Given a multidimensional response, a public manager will assess their levels of trust with the forum to determine how to behave. If the public manager has high levels of trust in the forum, they will be willing to be held to a higher level of accountability. If a public manager has low levels of trust, they will behave in defense bolstering. Given that a public manager does not expect that they will be held accountable for a specific act, they will engage in defense bolstering. Given defense bolstering, a public manager's level of trust in the forum will not be assessed as part of their response.

Anticipated accountability is necessary but not sufficient to get to responsiveness. Multidimensional thinking occurs when a trust verdict is reached about the forums. High trust is necessary and sufficient to get to responsiveness. Low trust is unnecessary but sufficient to get to defense bolstering. Unanticipated accountability is sufficient to get to defense bolstering.

While a public manager's level of trust may not affect their behavior in situations with unknown accountability, our research confirms two scenarios. The first scenario is one of dismissal of the forum's demands. The second scenario is an acknowledgment of the forum's demand and a willingness to change. It is in this second scenario that trust may emerge and restart the cycle of accountability. Further research is needed to confirm this hypothesis.

The initial formulation of the Calibrated Public Accountability Theory is steeped in policing. At present, policing is where routine and exceptional – and sometimes tragic – interactions are filmed. There is no clear reason why it must remain so. BWCs and other novel work surveillance technologies will change the ways accountability will be performed: "A 'theory' that cannot be arrow-diagrammed

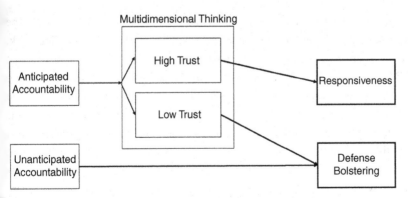

Figure 9 Parsimonious arrow-diagram of the Calibrated Public Accountability Theory

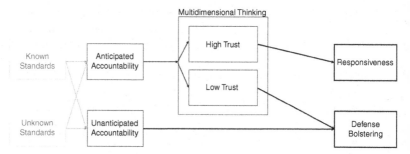

Figure 10 Complexified arrow-diagram of the Calibrated Public Accountability Theory

is not a theory, and needs reframing to become a theory" (Van Evera 1997, p. 18, emphasis in the original). Hence, we offer to the reader Figure 9.

In his CPA model, Schillimans (2016) puts much effort into discussing how well managers know standards of accountability ahead of time. We did not test that part of the CPA model. However, from an armchair position, we can think of scenarios where both known standards and unknown standards can lead to anticipated and unanticipated accountability alike. Stated differently, we think that known and unknown standards would be shaved off the theory with Occam's razor.

To be fair, "A clearly framed theory includes a statement about the antecedent conditions that enable its operation and govern its impact" (Van Evera 1997, p. 22). We believe that anticipated and unanticipated accountabilities are fitting starting points. We favor the parsimonious arrow-diagram of the calibrated public accountability theory illustrated in Figure 9 over the one in Figure 10. That being said, empirical examinations could settle the matters better than pure reasoning.

BWCs Outside of Policing

Video surveillance is already present in many other domains, occupations in the public sector among them, and BWCs remain but one way of recording work, along with cell phones, CCTV, dashboard cameras, drones, and satellites (Bowling and Iyer 2019, p. 148). One public domain where recording is gaining traction is education. So far, video surveillance for teachers takes the form of CCTV cameras in hallways and schoolyards and, more rarely, classrooms (Perry-Hazan and Birnhack 2019, p. 200). Some of the coping mechanisms available to teachers, like avoidance and concealment, would be harder to implement if they were eventually equipped with body-worn cameras, as there would not be "dead" areas – those not covered by cameras – where some teachers in Israel used to get a surveillance rest during their work days (Perry-Hazan and Birnhack 2019, p. 198).

In 2016, Steven Straus, a visiting professor at Princeton University, opined in the pages of the *Los Angeles Times* that the arguments in favor of the deployment of BWCs in policing are easily transferable to other fields. His main question is, "What's to limit this type of solution only to police officers?" (Straus 2016). He argues that, at present, Black students are suspended or expelled at three times the rates of white students. Parents and students are stuck in a case where it is a teacher's words against their own. A closer analogy to policing is health care, "another interaction which produces potentially life-or -death outcomes. In general, African Americans and other people of color receive inferior medical treatment, leading to higher death rates" (Straus 2016). Cameras, instead of physicians' words, would better document malpractice.

For now, researchers are coming to the realization that the existence of BWC footage is not enough to boost transparency, accountability, or legitimacy. In the absence of trust in the police by swaths of citizens, the concern expressed by officers that the absence of footage is indicative of a police cover-up that might grow (White and Malm 2020, p. 111). Cybersecurity threats could also undermine the confidence that citizens have in footage. Determined hackers could download footage, edit parts to fit a narrative, and upload a modified version; they could also delete footage entirely (White and Malm 2020, p. 114).

If the lack of trust endures, we can envision a world where the advent of deep fakes, the public release of BWC footage, or footage captured by a smartphone after a fatal shooting is no longer seen as objective proof. To explain why they did not find geographical differences in terms of general support from a nationally representative survey of 1,000 African Americans, Graham and colleagues speculated that it might be that:

> a national consensus has emerged among African Americans that law enforcement departments should, as a matter of good faith, equip officers with BWCs as one way to ensure constant accountability while officers are on patrol. . . . Police agencies that resist BWCs thus would be vulnerable to the charge that they have something to hide and, in turn, will lie to protect wayward officers. (Graham et al. 2019, p. 296)

Our research confirms a difference in perception between populations of color and white populations. Furthermore, based on this research and our broader observations of the use and misuse of BWCs, we conclude that BWC programs can lead to a number of outcomes. First, video footage opens a small window into the lived experience of persons of color, shedding light on injustices that Black and brown people experience daily. Hence, persons of color want that footage reviewed by an external source, not those with whom they have an untrustworthy relationship. Second, footage appeals to an uncomfortable voyeurism that represents the worst of our new viral social behavior, as evidenced by our findings that mental illness is not an acceptable reason for law enforcement to withhold footage. People's desire to see this footage suggests that we are less concerned with the law, and more concerned with viewing shocking events. Third, access to such footage creates a moment in time in which civilians can express outrage and demand a different type of policing. It is in this moment that progress will be achieved. Law enforcement agencies have a choice. They can dismiss that outrage and continue behaving in a manner that is out of step with the general public or they can acknowledge wrongdoings and change their behavior. As evidenced in our police narratives, many chiefs take this footage as an opportunity to "engage in just such transformative practices." Surveillance of police officers will not fix our problems. It will only pull at the thread in a fabric that is still being sewn or shift the rules and norms by which we hold one another accountable. One cannot use BWC footage to hold someone accountable for behavior that our norms and institutions have endorsed for more than 200 years. Our norms and institutions must change.

In polls, police officers remain among the most trusted public servants. Nevertheless, they are not trusted enough to use their discretion to do their job without being filmed. How long will other public servants, who are not trusted as much as cops, have before they must trade their professional discretion for a camera pinned to their chests?

References

Adams, Ian, & Mastracci, Sharon. (2019). Police Body-Worn Cameras: Development of the Perceived Intensity of Monitoring Scale. *Criminal Justice Review 44*(3), 386–405.

Alpert, Geoffrey P., & McLean, Kyle. (2018). Where Is the Goal Line? A Critical Look at Police Body-Worn Camera Programs. *Criminology & Public Policy, 17*(3), 679–688.

Ariel, Barak. (2019). Technology in Policing. In David Weisberg & Anthony A. Braga (Eds.), *Police Innovation: Contrasting Perspectives* (2nd ed., pp. 485–516). New York: Cambridge University Press.

Barnard, Chester I. (1938, 1968). *The Functions of the Executive.* Cambridge, MA: Harvard University Press.

Barrett, Michael. (2019, December 16). Surveillance Network Expands to More Gastonia, N.C., Parks. Gastonia, NC: *Gaston Gazette.*

Bartels, Koen. P. (2013). Public Encounters: The History and Future of Face-to-Face Contact Between Public Professionals and Citizens. *Public Administration, 91*(2), 469–483.

Bilodeau, É. (2019, October 3). Un hôpital contacte la police pour forcer un employé à travailler. Montréal, QC: La Presse.

Bogen, Miranda. (2018, March 1). What Happens to Body Cam Footage after Fatal Police Shootings? https://medium.com/equal-future/what-happens-to-body-cam-footage-after-fatal-police-shootings-7759606c5b20

Bovens, Mark. (2005). Accountability?(p. 182-208) In E. Ferlie, L. E. Lynn, & C. Pollitt (Eds.), *The Oxford Handbook of Public Management.* New York: Oxford University Press, 182–208.

(2007) Analysing and Assessing Accountability: A Conceptual Framework. *European Law Journal, 13*(4), 447–468.

(2010). Two Concepts of Accountability: Accountability as a Virtue and as a Mechanism. *West European Politics, 33*(5), 946–967.

Bowling, Ben, & Iyer, Shruti. (2019). Automated Policing: The Case of Body-Worn Video. *International Journal of Law in Context, 15*(1), 140–161.

Braga, Anthony A., Brunson, Rod K., & Drakulich, Kevin M. (2019). Race, Place, and Effective Policing. *Annual Review of Sociology, 45*, 535–555.

Braga, Anthony A., & Weisberg, David. (2019). Police Innovation and the Future of Policing. In David Weisberg & Anthony A. Braga (Eds.), *Police Innovation: Contrasting Perspectives* (2nd ed., pp. 544–563). New York: Cambridge University Press.

Braunstein, Rich, & Erickson, David. (2019). Best Practices, Challenges and Opportunities for Body Worn Camera Programs. *South Dakota Law Review*, *63*(3), 510–520.

Bromberg, Daniel E., Charbonneau, Étienne, & Smith, Andrew. (2018). Body-Worn Cameras and Policing: A List Experiment of Citizen Overt and True Support. *Public Administration Review*, *78*(6), 883–891.

Brooks, Rosa (2016). *How Everything Became War and the Military Became Everything: Tales from the Pentagon.* New York: Simon & Schuster.

Busuioc, Madalina E., and Lodge, Martin. (2016). The Reputational Basis of Public Accountability. *Governance* 29(2), 247–263.

Canadian Broadcasting Corporation. (2017, October 17th). Build Us a Body-Worn Camera with Technology 'That Doesn't Fail,' Toronto Police Tell Manufacturers. Toronto, ON: CBC News. http://www.cbc.ca/news/canada/toronto/toronto-body-worncameras-police-technology-1.4357773

Carr, James D., & Maxwell, Sheila Royo. (2018). Police Officers' Perceptions of Organizational Justice and Their Trust in the Public. *Police Practice and Research*, *19*(4), 365–379.

Charlotte-Mecklenburg Police Department. (2019). *Interactive Directives Guide – Body Worn Camera (BWC)*. Charlotte, NC: Charlotte-Mecklenburg Police Department. https://charlottenc.gov/CMPD/Documents/Resources/CMPDDirectives.pdf

Chavis, Kami. (2019). The Pitfalls of Police Technology: A Minority Report. In Tamara Rice Lave & Eric J. Miller (Eds.), *The Cambridge Handbook of Policing in the United States* (pp. 451–472). New York: Cambridge University Press.

Christensen, Tom, & Lægreid, Per. (2008). The Challenge of Coordination in Central Government Organizations: The Norwegian Case. *Public Organization Review*, *8*(2), 97–116.

(2011). Complexity and Hybrid Public Administration – Theoretical and Empirical Challenges. *Public Organization Review*, *11*(4), 407–423.

Christensen, Tom, Fimreite, Anne L., & Lægreid, Per. (2014). Joined-up Government for Welfare Administration Reform in Norway. *Public Organization Review*, *14*(4), 439–456.

Cotter, Adam. (2015). *Spotlight on Canadians: Results from the General Social Survey Public Confidence in Canadian Institutions.* Ottawa, ON: Statistics Canada.

Dahl, Robert A. (1947) The Science of Public Administration: Three problems *Public Administration Review*, 7(1), 1–11.

DeMarco, L. (2020). DC Police Union Suing over New Law that Mandates Release of Body Cam Video within 5 Days of Incident. Washington, DC: Fox 5 DC.

Dubnick, Melvin. (2002). Seeking Salvation from Accountability. Paper presented at the Annual Meeting of the American Political Science Association, Boston, MA.

(2005). Accountability and the Promise of Performance: In Search of the Mechanisms. *Public Performance & Management Review, 28*(3), 376–417.

Fan, Mary D. (2018a). Body Cameras, Big Data, and Police Accountability. *Law & Social Inquiry, 43*(4), 1236–1256.

(2018b). Democratizing Proof: Pooling Public and Police Body-Camera Videos. *North Carolina Law Review, 96*, 1639–1680.

Fox, Jonathan. (2007). The Uncertain Relationship Between Transparency and Accountability. *Development in Practice, 17*(4/5), 663–671.

Franks, Mary Anne (2017). Democratic Surveillance. *Harvard Journal of Law and Technology, 30*(2), 426–489.

Friedman, Barry. (2017). *Unwarranted: Policing Without Permission.* New York: Farrar, Straus and Giroux.

Gailmard, Sean. (2014). Accountability and Principal-Agent Models (pp. 90-105). In Mark Bovens, Robert Goodin, & Thomas Schillemans (Eds.), *Oxford Handbook of Public Accountability.* New York: Oxford University Press, 90–105.

Garvie, Clare, & Moy, Laura M. (2019). *America under Watch: Face Surveillance in the United States.* Washington, DC: Center on Privacy & Technology – Georgetown Law.

Gaub, Janne E., White, Michael D., Padilla, Kathleen E., & Katz, Charles M. (2017). *Implementing a Police Body-Worn Camera Program in a Small Agency.* Center for Violence Prevention and Community Safety. Tempe: Arizona State University.

Goodenow, Evan. (2018, July 19). No Crowd at Meetings on Winchester Police Body Cameras. Winchester, VA: *Winchester Star.* www.winchesterstar .com/news/winchester/no-crowd-at-meetings-on-winchester-police-body-cameras/article_b091c386-f7cc-5e7c-b814-d2a26a353cfe.html

Graham, Amanda, McManus, Hannah D. , Cullen, Francis T. , Burton, Velmer S. Jr., & Jonson, Cheryl Lero. (2019). Videos Don't Lie: African Americans' Support for Body-Worn Cameras. *Criminal Justice Review, 44*(3), 284–303.

Greiling, D., & Spraul, K. (2010). Accountability and the Challenges of Information Disclosure. *Public Administration Quarterly, 34*(3), 338–377.

Hagen, Christina S., Bighash, Leila, Hollingshead, Andrea B., Shaikh, Sonia Jawaid, & Alexander, Kristen S. (2018). Why Are You Watching? Video Surveillance in Organizations. *Corporate Communications: An International Journal, 23*(2), 274–291.

Halley, Meghan C., Rustagi, Alison S., Torres, Jeanette S., Linos, Elizabeth, Plaut, Victoria, Mangurian, Christina, . . . Linos, Eleni. (2018). Physician Mothers' Experience of Workplace Discrimination: A Qualitative Analysis. *British Medical Journal,* 363, 1–10.

Hamm, J., D'Annuzio, A. M., Bomstein, B. H., Hoetger, L., & Herian, M. N. (2019). Do Body-Worn Cameras Reduce Eyewitness Cooperation with the Police? An Experimental Inquiry. *Journal of Experimental Criminology,* 15(4), 685–701.

Han, Yousueng, & Perry, James L. (2020). Conceptual Bases of Employee Accountability: A Psychological Approach. *Perspectives on Public Management and Governance, 3*(4), 288–304.

Heald, David Albert. (2006). *Transparency: The Key to Better Governance?* Proceedings of the British Academy 135. New York: Oxford University Press, 25–43.

Hyland, Shelley. (2018). *Full-Time Employees in Law Enforcement Agencies, 1997–2016.* Washington, DC: US Department of Justice, Office of Justice Programs, Bureau of Justice Statistics.

Jennings, Wesley G., Fridell, Lorie A., & Lynch, Mathew.D. (2014). Cops and Cameras: Officer Perceptions of the Use of Body-Worn Cameras in Law Enforcement. *Journal of Criminal Justice, 42*(6), 549–556.

Jos, Philip H. (2006). Social Contract Theory: Implications for Professional Ethics. *The American Review of Public Administration, 36*(2), 139–155.

Judd, Alan. (2019, March 9). L.A.'s Gang-Tracking Database Offers Lessons to Others. Atlanta, GA: *Atlanta Journal-Constitution.*

Kääriäinen, Juha, & Sirén, Reino. (2012). Do the Police Trust in Citizens? European Comparisons. *European Journal of Criminology, 9*(3), 276–289.

Kayas, Oliver G., Hines, Tony, McLean, Rachel, & Wright, Gillian H. (2019). Resisting Government Rendered Surveillance in a Local Authority. *Public Management Review, 21*(8), 1170–1190.

Kofman, Ava. (2017, April 30). Taser will Use Police Body Camera Video "to Anticipate Criminal Activity." *The Intercept.*

Kohring, Matthias, and Matthes, Jörg (2007) Trust in News Media: Development and Validation of a Multidimensional Scale. *Communication Research* 34(2), 231–252.

Lannan, Katie. (2019, July 12). Mass. Police Warn Against Blanket Body Camera Rules. Worcester, MA: State House News Service. www.nepm .org/post/mass-bill-aims-exempt-body-camera-footage-public-record-laws#stream/0

Lawrence, Daniel S., McClure, David, Malm, Aili, Lynch, Mathew, & La Vigne, Nancy. (2019). Activation of Body-Worn Cameras: Variation by Officer, Over Time, and by Policing Activity. *Criminal Justice Review, 44* (3), 339–355.

Lambert, Alan J., Cronen, Stephanie, Alison L. Chasteen, & Lickel, Brian. (1996) Private vs Public Expressions of Racial Prejudice. *Journal of Experimental Social Psychology, 32*(5), 437–459.

Lerner, Jennifer S., & Tetlock, Philip E. (1999a). Accounting for the Effects of Accountability. *Psychological Bulletin, 125*(2), 255–275.

Lerner, Jennifer S., & Tetlock, Phillip E. (1999b). The Social Contingency Model: Identifying Empirical and Normative Boundary Conditions on the Error-and-Bias Portrait of Human Nature. In S. Chaiken & Y. Trope (Eds.), *Dual Process Theories in Social Psychology* (pp. 571–585). New York: Guilford Press.

Liebman, Brian. (2015). The Watchman Blinded: Does North Carolina Public Records Law Frustrate the Purpose of Police Body Worn Cameras. *North Carolina Law Review, 94*(1), 344–378.

Lipsky, Michael. (1980). *Street-Level Bureaucracy: Dilemmas of the Individual in Public Services*. New York: Russell Sage Foundation.

Livingston, James D. (2016) Contact between Police and People with Mental Disorders: A Review of Rates. *Psychiatric Services*, 67(8), 850–857.

Long, Jeremy. (2020, May 26). Reading, PA., Police Look to Purchase Body Cameras. Reading, PA: *Reading Eagle*. www.govtech.com/public-safety /Reading-Pa-Police-Look-to-Purchase-Body-Cameras.html

Los Angeles Police Department. (2015). Body Worn Video Procedures. Los Angeles, CA. http://assets.lapdonline.org/assets/pdf/body%20worn% 20camera.pdf Accessed 2020-01-14

Lum, Cynthia, & Gest, Ted. (2018). Progress and Prospects – The 50th Anniversary of the 1967 President's Crime Commission Report in Today's Criminal Justice Environment. *Criminology and Public Policy, 17*(2), 265–269.

Lum, Cynthia, Stoltz, Megan, Koper, Christopher S., & Scherer, J. Amber. (2019). Research on Body-Worn Cameras: What We Know, What We Need to Know. *Criminology & Public Policy, 18*(1), 93–118.

Macneil, Ian. (1986). Revisited: Individual Utility and Social Solidarity. *Ethics*, *96*(3), 567–593.

Maass, Arthur A., and Radway, Laurence I. (1949). Gauging Administrative Responsibility. *Public Administration Review*, 9(3), 182–193.

Maury, Kyle J. (2016). Police Body-Worn Camera Policy: Balancing the Tension Between Privacy and Public Access in State Laws. *Notre Dame Law Review*, 92(1), 479–512

McCluskey, John D., Uchida, Craig D., Solomon, Shellie E., Wooditch, Alese, Connor, Christine, & Revier, Lauren. (2019). Assessing the Effects of Body-Worn Cameras on Procedural Justice in the Los Angeles Police Department. *Criminology*, 57(2), 208–236.

McElroy, Laura. (2019a). *Embracing Communication with the Public and Media: A Key Component of a Successful Body-Worn Camera Program.* Tempe, AZ: Arizona State University.

McElroy, Laura. (2019b). *North Carolina's Body-Worn Camera Law Raises Questions.* Tempe, AZ: Arizona State University. www.bwctta.com /resources/commentary/view-north-carolinas-bwc-law

Merton, Robert K. (1940). Bureaucratic Structure and Personality. *Social Forces*, 560–568.

Miethe, Terance D., Lieberman, Joel D., Heen, Miliaikeala S. J., & Sousa, William H. (2019). Public Attitudes About Body-Worn Cameras in Police Work: A National Study of the Sources of Their Contextual Variability. *Criminal Justice Review*, 44(3), 263–283.

Miller, Ben. (2019, April 9). *What Body Cams Do: Policy, Discretion and Deeper Problems.* Folsom, CA: *Government Technology.* www.govtech .com/biz/data/What-Body-Cams-Do-Policy-Discretion-and-Deeper-Problems.html

Morris, Michael, & Moore, Paul. (1998) *Learning from a Brush with Danger: Evidence That Pilot Learning from Dangerous Incidents Is Enabled by Counterfactual Thinking and Hindered by Organizational Accountability.* Stanford Business School. Working paper No. 1492

Mounk, Yascha. (2018, June25). The Rise of McPolitics. New York: The New Yorker.

Mourtgos, Scott M., & Adams, Ian T. (2019). The Rhetoric of De-policing: Evaluating Open-Ended Survey Responses from Police Officers with Machine Learning-Based Structural Topic Modeling. *Journal of Criminal Justice*, 64, 61–73.

Mourtgos, Scott M., Mayer, Roger C., Wise, Richard A., and O'Rourke, Holly (2020) The Overlooked Perspective of Police Trust in the Public: Measurement and Effects on Police Job Behaviors. *Criminal Justice Policy Review*, 31(5), 639–672.

Mutz, Diana C. (2011). *Population-Based Survey Experiments*. Princeton, NJ: Princeton University Press.

Nadal, Kevin L., & Davidoff, Kristin C. (2015). Perceptions of Police Scale (POPS): Measuring Attitudes towards Law Enforcement and Beliefs about Police Bias. *Journal of Psychology and Behavioral Science*, *3*(2), 1–9.

National Academy of Public Administration. (2019). *Ensure Data Security and Individual Privacy*. The 12 Grand Challenges. Washington, DC. www.napawash.org/grandchallenges/challenge/ensure-data-security-and-individual-privacy

Newell, Bryce Clayton. (2014). Technopolicing, Surveillance, and Citizen Oversight: A Neorepublican Theory of Liberty and Information Control. *Government Information Quarterly*, *31*(3), 421–431.

Nix, Justin, & Pickett, Justin T. (2017). Third-Person Perceptions, Hostile Media Effects, and Policing: Developing a Theoretical Framework for Assessing the Ferguson Effect. *Journal of Criminal Justice*, *51*(1), 24–33.

Nix, Justin, Todak, Natalie, & Tregle, Brandon. (2020). Understanding Body-Worn Camera Diffusion in US Policing. *Police Quarterly*, 1098611120917937.

O'Kelly, Ciarán, & Dubnick, Melvin. (2014) *Accountability and Its Metaphors – From Forum to Agora and Bazaar*. 2014 EGPA Conference, Speyer, DE, 0–12.

Olsen, Johan. (2013). The Institutional Basis of Democratic Accountability. *West European Politics*, *36*(3): 447–473.

O'Neill, Onora. (2002). *A Question of Trust: The BBC Reith Lectures*. Cambridge: Cambridge University Press.

Overman, Sjors, Schillemans, Thomas, & Grimmelikhuijsen, Stephan. (2020). A Validated Measurement for Felt Relational Accountability in the Public Sector: Gauging the Account Holder's Legitimacy and Expertise. *Public Management Review*, 1–20.

Pagliarella, Chris. (2016). Police Body-Worn Camera Footage: A Question of Access. *Yale Law & Policy Review*, *34*(2), 533–543.

Parsons, Talcott. (1956). Suggestions for a Sociological Approach to the Theory of Organizations. II. *Administrative Science Quarterly*, *1*(2), 225–239.

Perry-Hazan, Lotem, & Birnhack, Michael. (2019). Caught on Camera: Teachers' Surveillance in Schools. *Teaching and Teacher Education*, *78*(1), 193–204.

Pew Research Center. (2018). *Americans' Confidence in U.S. Institutions*. Washington, DC: Pew Research Center.

Policing Project. (2018a). *Report to the Los Angeles Police Commission Summarizing Public Feedback on LAPD Video Release Policies.* New York: NYU School of Law.

——— (2018b). *Report to the NYPD Summarizing Public Feedback on Its Proposed Body-Worn Camera Policy.* New York: NYU School of Law.

Puente, Mark. (2018, October 2). LAPD Body Cams Help Exonerate Officers and Prove Misconduct. Los Angeles, CA: *Los Angeles Times.*

Rector, Kevin. (2019, May 22). Some of Baltimore's Citiwatch Cameras Aren't Working. Baltimore, MD: *Baltimore Sun.*

Reynolds, Christopher. (2019, December 12). Sea-Tac Pumps Brakes on Facial Recognition Testing. Los Angeles, CA: *Los Angeles Times.*

Roberts, John. (2009). No One Is Perfect: The Limits of Transparency and an Ethic for 'Intelligent' Accountability." *Accounting, Organizations and Society, 34*(8), 957–970.

Rodgers, Josh. (2015, September 25). State Releases Footage of North Country Police Shooting. NHPR. www.nhpr.org/post/state-releases-footage-north-country-police-shooting#stream/0

Romzek, Barbara S., & Dubnick, Melvin.J. (1987). Accountability in the Public Sector: Lessons from the Challenger Tragedy. *Public Administration Review, 47*(3), 227–238.

Schillemans, Thomas. (2013). The Public Accountability Review. A Meta-Analysis of Public Accountability Research in Six Academic Disciplines. Working Paper: Utrecht University School of Governance.

——— (2016). Calibrating Public Sector Accountability: Translating Experimental Findings to Public Sector Accountability. *Public Management Review, 18* (9), 1400–1420.

Schillemans, Thomas, & Bovens, Mark. (2011). The Challenge of Multiple Accountability: Does Redundancy Lead to Overload. In M. J. Frederickson (Ed.), *Accountable Governance: Problems and Promises* (pp. 3–21). Armonk, NY: ME Sharpe.

Schillemans, Thomas, & Busuioc, Madalina. (2015). Predicting Public Sector Accountability: From Agency Drift to Forum Drift. *Journal of Public Administration Research and Theory, 25*(1), 191–215.

Schlinkmann, Mark. (2020, June 17). St. Louis Police Could Start Using Body Cams by July. St. Louis, MO: St. Louis Post-Dispatch.

Seattle Information Technology. (2017). *Master List of Surveillance Technologies.* Seattle, WA: Seattle Information Technology. www.seattle.gov/Documents/Departments/SeattleIT/Master-List-Surveillance-Technologies.pdf

(2018). *Master List of Surveillance Technologies*. Seattle, WA.Seattle Information Technology. www.seattle.gov/Documents/Departments/ Tech/2018-09-28%20Revised%20Master%20List%20of%20Surveillance %20Technologies.pdf

Seattle Police Department. (2017). *Body-Worn Video Program*. Seattle, WA: Seattle Police Department. www.seattle.gov/police/about-us/body-worn -video

Sellick, Jared. (2019, October 3). Tampa Police Take Steps toward Transparency. Tampa, FL: The Oracle.

Sharkey, Patrick. (2018). *Uneasy Peace: The Great Crime Decline, the Renewal of City Life, and the Next War on Violence*. New York: W.W. Norton & Company.

Smith, Beth. (2019, September 21). Police Say Complaints Have Dropped Thanks to Body Cameras. Henderson, KY: *U.S. News & World Report*.

Smith, Justin J. (2019). To Adopt or Not to Adopt: Contextualizing Police Body-Worn Cameras Through Structural Contingency and Institutional Theoretical Perspectives. *Criminal Justice Review, 44*(3), 369–385.

Smoot, Sean. (2019). *In View Commentary: Body-Worn Cameras – Understanding the Union Perspective*. Body-Worn Camera – Trainning & Technical Assistance. Arizona State University. Tempe, AZ.

Smykla, John Ortiz, Crow, Matthew S., Crichlow, Vaughn J., & Snyder, Jamie A. (2016). Police Body-Worn Cameras: Perceptions of Law Enforcement Leadership. *American Journal of Criminal Justice, 41*(3) 424–443.

St. Louis, Ermus, Saulnier, Alana, & Walby, Kevin. (2019). Police Use of Body-Worn Cameras: Challenges of Visibility, Procedural Justice, and Legitimacy. *Surveillance & Society, 17*(3/4), 305–321.

Straus, Steven. (2016, April 4). Forget Cops. Should Doctors and Teachers Wear Body Cameras? Los Angeles, CA: *Los Angeles Times*.

Stroud, Matt. (2019). *Thin Blue Lie: The Failure of High-Tech Policing*. New York: Metropolitan Books.

Taylor, Emmeline. (2016). Lights, Camera, Redaction . . . Police Body-Worn Cameras; Autonomy, Discretion and Accountability. *Surveillance & Society* 14(1): 128–132.

Terrill, William, & Paoline, Eugene A. III. (2017). Police Use of Less Lethal Force: Does Administrative Policy Matter? *Justice Quarterly, 34*(2), 193–216.

Tetlock, Philip E. (1992). The Impact of Accountability on Judgment and Choice: Toward a Social Contingency Model. *Advances in Experimental Social Psychology*, 25(3), 331–376.

(1999). Accountability Theory: Mixing Properties of Human Agents with Properties of Social Systems. In J. M. Levine, D.M. Messick, & L. L. Thompson (Eds.) *Shared Cognition in Organizations: The Management of Knowledge.* (pp. 117–137). East Sussex, UK: Psychology Press.

Tetlock, Philip E., Skitka, Linda, & Boettger, Richard. (1989). Social and Cognitive Strategies for Coping with Accountability: Conformity, Complexity, and Bolstering. *Journal of Personality and Social Psychology, 57*(4), 632–640.

Thibaut, John, & Kelley, Harold. (1959). *The Social Psychology of Groups.* New York: Wiley.

Thompson, Daniel M. (2019). *Do Elections Increase Local Policy Responsiveness? Evidence from Elected Police Commissioners.* Stanford, CA: Stanford University.

Tolbert, Caroline J., & Mossberger, Karen. (2006). The Effects of e-Government on Trust and Confidence in Government. *Public Administration* Review, *66*(3), 354–369.

Tregle, Brandon, Nix, Justin, & Pickett, Justin T. (2020). Body-Worn Cameras and Transparency: Experimental Evidence of Inconsistency in Police Executive Decision-Making. *Justice Quarterly,* 1–23.

Turner, Broderick L., Caruso, Eugene M., Dilich, Mike A., & Roese, Neal J. (2019). Body Camera Footage Leads to Lower Judgments of Intent Than Dash Camera Footage. *Proceedings of the National Academy of Sciences of the United States of America, 116*(4), 1201–1206.

Turner, Frederick W. II, & Fox, Bryanna Hahn. (2019). Public Servants or Police Soldiers? An Analysis of Opinions on the Militarization of Policing from Police Executives, Law Enforcement, and Members of the 114th Congress U.S. House of Representatives. *Police Practice and Research, 20*(2), 122–138.

Uchida, Craig D., Haas, Robert, & Solomon, Shellie E. (2019). *In View Commentary: Releasing BWC Video to the Public: Policy Implications.* Arizona State University. Tempe, AZ.

Upturn. (2017). *Police Body Worn Cameras: A Policy Scorecard.* November. Washington, DC: Leadership Conference on Civil and Human Rights. www.bwcscorecard.org/

Urban Institute. (2018, October 29). *Police Body-Worn Camera Legislation Tracker.* Washington, DC: Urban Institute. http://apps.urban.org/features/body-camera-update/

Van de Walle, Steven, & Lahat, Lihi. (2017). Do Public Officials Trust Citizens? A Welfare State Perspective. *Social Policy & Administration, 51*(7), 1450–1469.

Van Evera, Stephan. (1997). *Guide to Methods for Students of Political Science.* Ithaca, NY: Cornell University Press.

Vitale, Alex.S. (2018). *The End of Policing.* Brooklyn, NY: Verso.

Watson Fisher, Jadyn. (2018, January 8). Seized Money Will Help Pay for One City's Police Body Cams. Fort Smith, AK: *Times Record.* www .govtech.com/public-safety/Seized-Money-Will-Help-Pay-for-One-Citys -Police-Body-Cams.html

White, Michael D., Gaub, Janne E., Malm, Aili, & Padilla, Kathleen E. (2019). Implicate or Exonerate? The Impact of Police Body-Worn Cameras on the Adjudication of Drug and Alcohol Cases. *Policing,* 1–11.

White, Michael D., & Malm, Aili. (2020). *Cops, Cameras, and Crisis: The Potential and the Perils of Police Body-Worn Cameras.* New York: New York University Press.

Worden, Robert E., & McClean, Sarah J. (2017). *Mirage of Police Reform: Procedural Justice and Police Legitimacy.* Oakland: University of California Press.

Worthy, Ben. (2010). More Open but Not More Trusted? The Effect of the Freedom of Information Act 2000 on the United Kingdom Central Government. *Governance, 23*(4), 561–582.

Wright, James E. II, & Headley, Andrea M. (2020). Can Technology Work for Policing? Citizen Perceptions of Police-Body Worn Cameras. *American Review of Public Administration,* 51(1), 17-27.

Yang, Kaifeng. (2005). Public Administrators' Trust in Citizens: A Missing Link in Citizen Involvement Efforts. *Public Administration Review, 65*(3), 273–285.

(2006). Trust and Citizen Involvement Decisions: Trust in Citizens, Trust in Institutions, and Propensity to Trust. *Administration & Society, 38*(5), 573–595.

Acknowledgments

We thank the hundreds of police chiefs who answered our two surveys. We thank Rémi Boivin, for graciously sharing the BWC training videos with us. We thank Kimberly Mitchell at the Crimes against Children Research Center, University of New Hampshire, for sharing the Police Bureau database. We thank Alasdair Roberts, for the encouragements and pieces of advice he offered in a Baltimore pub about writing a book. We thank Melvin Dubnick, Alexander Henderson, Karina Moreno, Jessica Sowa, Edmund Stazyk, and Gregg Van Ryzin for the comments they offered on the manuscript. We thank all of the others who have reviewed this manuscript, anonymous or otherwise. Your comments were greatly appreciated. We thank Madeleine Rousseau and Brennan Pouliot for their research assistance. Étienne Charbonneau acknowledges funding from the Canada Research Chairs program. We acknowledge Canada's Social Sciences and Humanities Research Council support through Insight grant (#435–2020-1013). We thank Robert Christensen and Andy Whitford, the editors of this series, for this opportunity.

Cambridge Elements ☰

Public and Nonprofit Administration

Andrew Whitford
University of Georgia

Andrew Whitford is Alexander M. Crenshaw Professor of Public Policy in the School of Public and International Affairs at the University of Georgia. His research centers on strategy and innovation in public policy and organization studies.

Robert Christensen
Brigham Young University

Robert Christensen is professor and George Romney Research Fellow in the Marriott School at Brigham Young University. His research focuses on prosocial and antisocial behaviors and attitudes in public and nonprofit organizations.

About the Series

The foundations of this series are cutting-edge contributions on emerging topics and definitive reviews of keystone topics in public and nonprofit administration, especially those that lack longer treatment in textbook or other formats. Among keystone topics of interest for scholars and practitioners of public and nonprofit administration, it covers public management, public budgeting and finance, nonprofit studies, and the interstitial space between the public and nonprofit sectors, along with theoretical and methodological contributions, including quantitative, qualitative and mixed-methods pieces.

The Public Management Research Association

The Public Management Research Association improves public governance by advancing research on public organizations, strengthening links among interdisciplinary scholars, and furthering professional and academic opportunities in public management.

Cambridge Elements $\equiv$

Public and Nonprofit Administration

Printed in the United States
by Baker & Taylor Publisher Services